# Get Me the Urgent Biscuits

# Get Me the Urgent Biscuits

· · · · · · · · · · · · · · · · · · · · · · · ·

*An Assistant's Adventures
in Theatreland*

SWEETPEA SLIGHT

WEIDENFELD & NICOLSON

First published in Great Britain in 2017
by Weidenfeld & Nicolson
an imprint of The Orion Publishing Group Ltd
Carmelite House, 50 Victoria Embankment
London EC4Y 0DZ
An Hachette UK Company

1 3 5 7 9 10 8 6 4 2

A CIP catalogue record for this book is
available from the British Library.

ISBN (Hardback) 978 1 474 60519 9

Typeset by Input Data Services Ltd, Somerset

www.orionbooks.co.uk

*For the indomitable Thelma Holt*

# Contents

# Contents

# Prologue

By the time I opened the small black box and read the little card, my last day was already behind me. In the morning I would begin the first day for twenty years without her. It was 2 a.m. As I stepped out of the taxi Thelma pressed something small and hard into my hand, telling me not to open it until the morning. Well, it was the morning and my curiosity was too great. The box, which was black plastic, contained a gold brooch: two conjoined hearts – much like a Mizpah. The inscription read: *The Lord watch between me & thee when we are absent one from another*. The little card that had been held tightly round the box with an old elastic band read simply: *cry you cunt! xxxx*.

I didn't cry. I was beyond the frivolity of tears. It felt like a coming-of-age sadness, a deep numb thing that would take a while to evaporate. I knew Thelma wouldn't cry. She had cried only once in the time I'd spent with her and that was when her cat Shiva died. She was inconsolable then.

# 1

## *Dolly Dots*

I was eighteen when I first met Thelma Holt. It was 1984; I had just finished A levels and was on work experience at the Theatre of Comedy, en route, or so I thought, to Drama School, where I had plans to become the next Helen Mirren.

My parents had driven me to London in their old white Saab 96, delivering me and my two holdalls to a hostel in Bloomsbury. Apparently I couldn't wait to get rid of them, I was so excited. A new life beckoned and neither fear nor doubt had yet emerged in my psyche. They had moved from London to Dorset when I was eight, having bought a run-down old farmhouse into which they sank almost all their money. Although there was an indoor flushable loo, the bath was conspicuous by its absence. For eighteen months we bathed in a tin trough in front of an old log burner so inefficient that it devoured logs at an unbelievable rate. There was no television until I was sixteen.

The Theatre of Comedy had been formed the year before by Ray Cooney, farceur and director. Thelma had been wooed by Ray to join the company as Executive Producer to expand the remit of the company – a wise appointment. For the previous seven years she had run the Roundhouse in Chalk Farm very successfully with Robert Maxwell as Treasurer. She later told me that in their first meeting he'd entered the room saying, 'I'm

Robert Maxwell, there are three things you need to know about me – I don't drink, I don't gamble and I don't sleep with women', to which Thelma had replied, 'Mr Maxwell, how splendid, at least we have two things in common.'

The Theatre of Comedy didn't really produce the kind of work Thelma would become known for. But her eye was focused on the opportunity to produce Joe Orton's *Loot* with Leonard Rossiter. Thelma loved Joe Orton and this play in particular. Indeed, the production sold out during its initial run at the Ambassadors Theatre and transferred to the Lyric on Shaftesbury Avenue. A week later Thelma was at the Ambassadors Theatre, where another Theatre of Comedy production had recently opened. She was sitting on the floor in the bar having a drink with Malcolm, her deputy and amanuensis, when she received a call from the Lyric. She says she will never forget running down Shaftesbury Avenue with Malcolm trailing behind her. She shouted to him over her shoulder, 'If that fucking company manager is wrong I'm going to kill him.' By the time she reached the theatre, Leonard was dead. He had died in his dressing room just as he was due to go on stage.

On my first day at the Theatre of Comedy, Thelma wasn't there. I wasn't to know at the time, but she was in the United States giving evidence in Vanessa Redgrave's suit against the Boston Symphony Orchestra. They had cancelled her contract to narrate Stravinsky's *Oedipus Rex* because of her support for the Palestine Liberation Organisation. Malcolm told me some time later that Thelma had received a call from Vanessa saying, 'Can you come, I need you.' Thelma replied, 'When do you want me?' 'Now,' said Vanessa.

\*

I had come to see the Financial Director in the hope that I would be given work in the theatre, backstage. He explained that this wouldn't be possible because of union regulations and instead offered me work in the office, with the Marketing Department. He asked if I was free to work that evening to help out in the theatre bar with an after-performance event in the Shaftesbury Theatre, where Ray Cooney's production of *Two into One* was performing. I said yes.

He looked me up and down; he might have thought my dress sense was a little odd. I was wearing plus-fours and brogues, a shirt and cardigan – smart, I thought – but I sensed he was appalled. I had a bob haircut and painted freckles on my face – across my nose and cheeks. I was very good at applying these and nobody had ever questioned their authenticity. I was five feet ten inches and slender, physical characteristics that bothered me, and the confidence suggested by my eccentric attire was at odds with the reality. I was fair-haired, blue-eyed, with an English rose complexion. One of my mother's friends had once given me a large badge that said 'luscious peach'. I didn't feel like a luscious peach, more like a gawky, awkward foal. Had I 'a frock'? he asked. I didn't, but again said yes.

As soon as I left him I headed straight to the nearest clothes shop on the corner of Oxford Street where I bought a skirt, a new top and cardigan. I had to wear the brogues, though; the budget couldn't run to new shoes as well. I probably looked odder still.

Returning to the office that evening, I met a very smiley, polished, enthusiastic and confident woman, who ran the Marketing Department. She was incredibly nice and explained that all I would have to do was hand drinks around and smile. She even organised my seat to watch the performance from. I'd never seen a farce and remember feeling oddly detached from it. Aware that the actors were 'performing' – however brilliantly they carried it off and however funny it was – I found it hard to become involved.

The theatre I had fallen in love with started with a trip to see a production of Brecht's *The Caucasian Chalk Circle*. Despite the isolated location of home during my childhood, Mum and Dad would seek out any film or play and drive miles to make sure we saw it. So when the Royal Shakespeare Company announced a visit to Yeovil, tickets were booked weeks in advance.

It was the first time I had seen live theatre. These actors, who brought words to life, were not like other human beings to me. They were special, defying ordinariness with their transformative powers. Later, during a school trip to Stratford-upon-Avon where we camped for a week, I'd seen *A Doll's House* with Cheryl Campbell playing Nora, and *King Lear* with Michael Gambon, and Antony Sher as his Fool. My London theatre trips included the Royal Shakespeare Company's Greek cycle of plays at the Aldwych (I only got to see part two – *The Murders*). I bought the music on cassette and back in Dorset would play it on my very cheap tape recorder in the confines of my bedroom while summoning up images of Janet Suzman's Clytemnestra and John Shrapnel's Agamemnon.

All these productions stayed with me for weeks. I felt lonely in Stratford because nobody else seemed to be as upset as I was about Lear and his Fool, or indeed about Nora. As we stood outside The Other Place – the small studio theatre in Stratford where we had just seen

*A Doll's House* – everyone was excitedly off into town to get late-night fish and chips. I was appalled; how could they possibly go and eat fish and chips after what we had just seen! My English teacher looked at me with understanding.

Cooney's plays were very clever, and the original cast was impressive: Donald Sinden and Michael Williams. The audiences loved it, and although Thelma could be dismissive of these customers and never subscribed to coach-party marketing, she did acknowledge its potential benefit. But I would never come to terms with farce. *Wife Begins at Forty* and *Run for Your Wife* were typical examples of the Cooney title talent. What I did love was being in the theatre and being involved, even in what was then a very small way. I didn't know technically how productions worked. I didn't know the difference between a director and a producer, I didn't know what a stage manager did. I would remain ignorant of everything until Thelma appeared.

In those days I would blush if a pin dropped. I'd get a big perfectly round red mark on each cheek and these would eventually be referred to by Thelma as my 'dolly dots'. Coupled with the freckles, it gave me the appearance of someone younger than eighteen. I had to carry a photocopy of my birth certificate until well into my twenties, as I was regularly refused alcohol in bars. The dolly dots bothered me more than I ever admitted and sabotaged my confidence. The application of face powder usually looked as if a bag of flour had exploded in my face and still the red broke through. My paternal Grandma Peggie was a beautician who through one of her contacts at Estée Lauder sourced a light foundation to suit my childlike complexion. Though I put too much on, the total white-out was a comfort as it really hid my fierce blushes.

Any kind of overexcitement or nervousness would bring on the dolly dots and they were most evident that night. One of the leading actors, Michael Williams, went out of his way to come and talk to me. I suspect he sensed my awkwardness and felt sympathetic towards me in my odd attire, struggling through the crowded bar with a tray full of drinks. Chewing on his pipe, he wanted to know where I had come from and what my job was, and seemed impressed to hear that my new-found work experience was part of a plan to prepare me for applying to drama school. Our chat was short-lived as he was soon monopolised by a new collection of fans. I didn't know anything about him, but he was the first actor I had ever met in real life following a performance. He wasn't a tall man, his face was kind and handsomely creased, he was impish. Someone told me later that he was married to another actor called Judi Dench.

For the next two or three weeks my life fell into a particular pattern. I would arrive at the office at 10 a.m. and sit in a boardroom on my own with half a dozen very large grey post office sacks full of returned Comedy Club mail-outs. I had to open each envelope, separate the contents, keep certain parts and bin the rest. I didn't understand the purpose of any of it. Clutching a copy of the *London A–Z*, I would then make deliveries around the city, go and buy lunch for the team, make cups of tea and coffee, and carry out other jobs that were beneath the skills of those more elaborately employed. At lunchtime I would take over on the switchboard to allow the woman who worked it to have her break. It was one of those very old-fashioned instruments with a lot of buttons and lights and I was given fairly basic instruction on how to operate it, which meant I would often accidentally leave callers in the system for some time or indeed cut them off completely.

At least once a week I would be asked to go over the road to the Shaftesbury Theatre to photocopy a script. In the Theatre Manager's office at the very top of the building was a Xerox machine the size of a small car. It took an inordinate amount of time to copy each page: lifting the heavy lid to place the paper on the glass, replacing the lid, pressing the button and waiting for the thing to whirr then slide from right to left. Staying focused on such a dull task required particular attention, and I quickly worked out the fastest way to process each page – which involved lifting the lid to remove and replace pages at speed while the green light blinded me. I would return to the office with a kaleidoscope of green lines obscuring my vision that would take the rest of the day to dissolve.

At six o'clock the glamorous painted ladies in the Marketing Department would open a bottle of white wine. I remember the dimmed lights, the popping of corks, the applying of even more lipstick, behind all of which lurked a miasma of middle-aged disappointment. The apotheosis of this was one particular secretary, a woman who appeared to reek of regret. It seemed to me that the presence of a young fresh-faced and attractive girl at the beginning of her career elicited, perhaps against her better judgement, a distinct lack of generosity of spirit.

I met Malcolm a week before I would meet Thelma. He was in the bar of the Shaftesbury one evening drinking miniature bottles of vodka with the Company Accountant and a man they called Pearl, who was the Wardrobe Master. I listened to these three camp men bitch about someone called Thelma (I didn't know what camp was, and I couldn't understand the colourful way they spoke to one another). It seemed the woman, Thelma, who was this poor man Malcolm's boss, was awful and made his life a misery. I must have looked very serious when I asked him why he stayed, to which he replied, 'Oh, I love her, she drives me crazy, but I love her.'

I didn't know it then, but I know now that Malcolm looks like Alan Cumming's character Eli Gold in *The Good Wife*. When I first got to know him he wore jumbo cords, suede desert boots, checked shirts and V-neck sweaters. The cords were later replaced with jeans, the desert boots became sensible black shoes. Otherwise, little changed. Malcolm was to become my 'go-to' person for enlightenment on all the things I didn't understand. He was very kind and supportive to me in those early days. It seems ridiculous now that I was so naive, so unworldly. In some ways my ignorance was a blessing; I had no fear of anything. As Orson Welles famously said, 'There is a great gift that ignorance has to bring to anything.'

Location-wise, I'd landed on my feet. Our offices were directly opposite the Shaftesbury Theatre. I lived a five-minute walk away on Great Russell Street. Helen Graham House was the newly refurbished Young Women's Christian Association and was full of young girls, either at university, looking for work, or on some kind of apprenticeship. It was also, rather sadly, home to a number of older, less fortunate women.

My parents thought the hostel the best place for me to base myself, and during my brief time there I made a lot of friends and it was more fun than it might sound to live in such a place. The rent was £35 per week. There were shared bathrooms on each floor, though the rooms were all equipped with a small sink. Other than that, you got a single bed, a desk, some shelves, a wardrobe and a chair. There was a pay phone on every level and messages would be left in pigeonholes. In the basement the kitchens were arranged in a quadrant and coordinated according to your floor level. We were provided with little lockable crates that fitted into the fridges and lockable cupboards. I had a room with a large bay window that overlooked the centre of the British Museum. I couldn't believe my luck. At night it lit up like a film set. On Sundays I could walk the few hundred yards and feast my eyes upon the letters of literary greats, or the Egyptian mummies.

I made friends immediately with two girls on my floor. Scarlett from Oldham was studying archaeology at UCL and Nina was a dental student. Nina rather luxuriously owned a television, which meant never having to go down to the depressing institution-like lounge on the ground floor.

Perhaps the most extraordinary thing about the hostel was that Thelma had lived in exactly the same place when she first came to London to attend RADA, and she too had occupied a room on the front, overlooking the museum. She told me how she and her room-mate had cried the day Ruth Ellis was hanged, and they watched a woman chain herself to the gates of the British Museum in protest.

# 2

## *Which One of You Is Helen Mirren?*

I imagine it would be impossible today for any eighteen-year-old to be as unworldly as I was then. There were no computers or mobile phones and having spent most of my childhood without a television, I wasn't even streetwise by proxy. London was a stimulating and challenging dream, and as though in a movie, with no expectation other than the day-to-day, there came an inflated sense of promise.

It felt as though having left the family home I had been adopted into another kind of happy family. I had always been drawn to the eccentric, the world of make-believe and the imagination, and I was too enthralled to question that the reality of the theatre might not necessarily live up to the pretence. Furthermore, my innocence was a default form of protection insofar as I seemed fearless. Staggering around Tottenham Court Road late one night, hideously drunk and incapable of finding my way to the hostel, I was stopped by an Underground worker who kindly set me in the right direction. The following morning I recalled his look of concern and shuddered.

The life I had just come from was sheltered, mostly by dint of geography, and the majority of my life experiences to date had been vicarious. My father was a sculptor, my mother a painter. They both taught part-time in art colleges, which was how most practising artists survived in those days. My mother also ran her own small and successful leather accessories business. Having run out of old council-owned derelict buildings to turn into studio spaces, it was a book about self-sufficiency by John Seymour which galvanised them into leaving London and heading for the countryside, embracing his philosophy to the point of buying a Jersey cow, which Mum milked every day. There followed a veritable menagerie.

Dorset at that time wasn't full of incomers. Nor was it trendy to live the self-sufficient life, so I think the locals must have thought us rather eccentric. Although these days I am sure it is less uncommon for children to have their mother's home-made cheese with its accompanying straw and very particular odour, whole tomatoes and last night's leftover lasagne in their lunch box, believe me, it was unheard of in 1973.

I had gone from a very good primary school in London to a knit-one-drop-one village school in Dorset, where I went backwards. Mum and Dad did their best to ameliorate this with home education. Whatever they were doing, they would always make time to have a cup of tea with my younger brother Hodie and me when we arrived after the school bus had dropped us at the top of the track. We'd have tea and cake and tell them about our day, what we had learnt – which at this particular establishment was very little.

One day they found us uncharacteristically quiet, but could tell we were bursting with some very exciting news. It didn't take long for us to pour out the day's events: 'Stanley Cook hanged Myrtle Swan!' we shouted excitedly. 'She had to be cut down from the porch roof!'

Stanley Cook was the kind of clever boy who made radios out of Oxo boxes. That morning, in the first break, he had asked me for my finger in order to demonstrate how to tie a hangman's knot. Later, someone else had been dragged round the playground by their leg, and by lunchtime, unbeknown to anyone, he had perfected his hangman's noose. He then somehow persuaded Myrtle to let him hang her from the porch rafters. Suffering terrible shock and a sore neck – but fortunately discovered almost immediately – she was taken off to the school nurse. Miles was whacked with a plimsoll.

Secondary school was an improvement but Hodie and I still seemed marked out as aliens. We were already considered odd, speaking with different accents, and dressed in unusual clothes; I was three or four inches taller than most girls my age, and very skinny. I grew so quickly in the first couple of years at secondary school that Mum, rather than buying new trousers, would stitch strips of material to the bottom of my blue corduroys; by the time there were three strips I felt very embarrassed, particularly when she decided that a piece of leather would ring the changes. Worse, the washing machine did terrible things to the leather, which turned hard and wrinkly. I was delighted when Mum finally admitted defeat and got me a new pair of trousers.

Several times a year Mum would get up at 5 a.m. and milk the cow before catching a train to London with her leather samples to visit buyers from the USA. Dad would then be left to struggle with the daily domesticity. Despite carefully written instructions, he would often be unable to find crucial kit, like our lunch boxes – which Mum would have prepared in advance. 'Where are they?' he'd say accusingly. 'Where are what?' 'Your black plastics!' We had no idea what he was talking about, until he boomed, 'Your feed tubs!'

Invariably we would miss the school bus. This in turn meant him chasing it at high speed in his beat-up old Land Rover, banging on his horn and waving out of the window, until the coach driver (unbelievably named Walter Pigeon) would stop. I hated this because it attracted even more attention. When it came to home time we were the only children whose father collected them from the school gates in a welding suit with goggles perched on the top of his head, waving his arms and shouting, 'Over here, kids!' as if we hadn't already spotted him in the Land Rover. Hodie and I just wanted him to drive a Ford Granada and wear a shirt and tie and wait for us in the car, like all the other dads.

The phrase 'pissed off with your father' was often heard when Mum returned from one of these trips to find any number of favourite things missing from the house. Her much-loved *coeur à la crème* dish (white heart-shaped porcelain) purchased from the Elizabeth David Cookshop in 1965 and sold to her personally by the late great Elizabeth, was incorporated into one of Dad's sculptures. It had been filled with molten aluminium and the resultant cracked and distorted heart formed the centrepiece of a large installation.

When we moved to Dorset our parents had decided not to replace the television, a situation that persisted until I was sixteen. Instead they took us on occasion to the local film society to see subtitled foreign films and old Buster Keaton movies, or the latest releases at the local 1930s cinema. This was where we saw *Jaws*, but there was a moratorium for some time after that trip because I wouldn't go to the loo unaccompanied and had to check under the bed for weeks afterwards. (The shark problem followed me to London, where aged twenty-two I was rescued from a pool in the Porchester Baths by a burly young Australian. 'What happened?' he asked when I'd finished spitting out chlorinated water. I could hardly tell him that I had seen a great white break through the vent in the deep end of the pool.)

I devoured books and lived in the world of whatever novel I was reading, believing the characters to exist outside the pages; I would speak their language and live in their houses. The rare film I was allowed to see had an enormous impact on me, particularly any film of a book I had loved. When my parents took me to see John Schlesinger's *Far from the Madding Crowd*, which had been filmed all round where we lived, I went into a state of grace for six weeks (my mother counted). Fed up with seeing me standing in a field staring at Eggardon Hill, wondering where Bathsheba and Sergeant Troy were, and equally Julie Christie and Terence Stamp, my mother stood in front of me, clicked her fingers and said, 'If you don't snap out of this brown study soon, young lady, I'm going to have to veto films for good.'

I cried for days after *Gone with the Wind* and went into a decline after *A Streetcar Named Desire*. Mum refused to drive me to Lyme Regis after I'd seen *The French Lieutenant's Woman* – 'I'm not having you standing on the Cobb staring out to sea – you need to pull yourself together – we're not having another *Far from the Madding Crowd* moment!' *The Go-Between* discombobulated me and so did Julie Christie. 'The past is a foreign country, they do things differently there,' I announced wistfully in the face of Mum's wrath when she discovered I had eaten two whole raw Christmas puddings she had stored in the pantry, having thought this crime would go unnoticed. With the help of a god-mother, Mum's original creations were replaced with versions from Fortnum's, but my casual literary rebuttal annoyed Mum more than the bizarre scoffing of the puddings.

To make up for the lack of a television, as a family we would sometimes go to friends' houses to watch films on TV. I remember sitting on the floor in someone's living room watching *El Cid*, starring Charlton Heston and Sophia Loren. Hodie had never seen anyone like her. 'Mum, why is that lady wearing plastic lips?'

But these occasions were few and far between. Most of the time, if we weren't reading, we were listening to plays on the radio, and this is where my fascination with theatre began. One summer's day we sat around the kitchen table listening to the radio for the final episode of *Les Misérables*. As it concluded to the strains of Berlioz's Symphonie Fantastique we all burst into tears – at which point the door opened and in walked an American friend of my parents who had just driven from London. She took one look at us, dropped her bags and exclaimed, 'Oh no! What's happened?'

In those days plays were still shown on television as part of the BBC's *Play of the Month* series, and this was when I really started to cherish drama and to appreciate for the first time the work of particular actors. Michael Kitchen in Stephen Poliakoff's *Caught on a Train*, Kate Nelligan in David Hare's *Dreams of Leaving*. Best of all was Helen Mirren as Rosalind in *As You Like It*, and then in the films *The Long Good Friday* and *Cal*.

*

I took these growing passions with me when I left home and they began to blossom at the Theatre of Comedy. I was delighted when soon after starting there I was given the opportunity to see Helen Mirren perform in a play called *Extremities*.

The Theatre of Comedy was co-producing this at the Duchess Theatre. Despite her name (she had not quite reached the stratospheric levels of her current fame), the production was not selling out, so I was used as a seat filler, something I considered the greatest privilege.

*Extremities* was a play about a rape. I remember there were very violent scenes and I didn't particularly like the production. Indeed, in my then very inexperienced opinion, I didn't think it was very good. But none of that mattered because I was watching Helen Mirren live on stage, just feet away from me, and here was the magic hitherto solely experienced on screen. I forgot that she was Helen Mirren – she was 'Marjorie', the victim of the assault. I walked back to Great Russell Street through Covent Garden with dreams of becoming the next Helen Mirren. I wrote her a letter and on three consecutive nights walked to the theatre and tried to pluck up courage to leave it for her at the stage door, but each time I returned to the hostel with the letter undelivered.

I had never met one of my idols before, only coming close on a trip to London aged fourteen. My mum was seeing buyers for her leather goods in Harrods, I was told to wait for her at the cheese counter in the food hall, 'Right here by the Stilton,' she said strictly – pointing at it through the glass. At the appointed hour I made my way to the cheese counter. Suddenly I saw, coming towards the opposite side of the cheese counter, Lauren Bacall. I had watched *The Big Sleep*, *To Have and Have Not* and *Key Largo* and wanted to look like Lauren Bacall. My copy of Lauren Bacall's autobiography, *By Myself*, had been confiscated during a physics class.

I couldn't believe it, Lauren Bacall buying cheese. By the time Mum arrived she had gone. 'Mum! Lauren Bacall was here buying cheese!' 'Don't be silly,' she said. 'Come on or we will miss our train.'

On the third night waiting outside the stage door, my friend Scarlett accompanied me; she fancied the walk. We were just about to cross the road when Helen Mirren appeared with members of the cast and began walking up Catherine Street. Despite Scarlett's pushing and prodding, I wouldn't approach her. We followed them up the street and watched them disappear into an Indian restaurant.

Well, that's that again, I thought. But Scarlett snatched the letter from me saying 'For fuck's sake!' and disappeared inside the restaurant. I turned and began to walk back down the street. About two or three minutes later Scarlett re-emerged. To my horror she had approached the table and demanded, 'Which one of you is Helen Mirren?' and when Helen made herself known said, 'My friend has written you this letter and has been hanging around for fucking days plucking up the courage to give it to you, so here it is.'

We had just turned the corner at the bottom of the street when I heard someone shouting. I ignored this initially, thinking it nothing to do with me. It got louder and I heard my name. We turned to see Helen Mirren running down the road waving what appeared to be my letter in the air. I stood rooted to the spot until she reached us.

Much smaller in real life than on stage, she possessed something that Stanislavsky wrote about in *An Actor Prepares*. Often great actors who appear physically impressive on stage are much smaller when we meet them, but still have the charisma, which gives them magnificence both on and off stage and sets them apart. Others, despite their considerable talents and charisma on stage, may become invisible off. I was stunned to find that 'Marjorie', who had spent most of the evening in a dressing gown, had turned back into Helen Mirren and was now before me in jeans and a leather jacket, and for me cloaked in an effortless aura of stardom.

She said slightly breathlessly, 'Are you . . . ?'

'Yes,' I said.

'You've written me this beautiful letter and you didn't put your address on it – I might never have found you.'

Her generosity in abandoning her guests for a good twenty minutes in order to walk me round the block and tell me there were many ways to approach the business was something I have never forgotten. We exchanged addresses and a week later a letter arrived at the hostel containing two brand-new twenty-pound notes, one for Scarlett and one for me. She said she well remembered life as a student in London and instructed that the enclosed was 'for fun'.

We celebrated at the Barocco Bar in Soho, it was cheap, and one of the very few places we could afford. We took our own wine and it was easy to become giddy with a sense of how vibrant life felt. We ordered cheesecake and Sambuca – I'd never heard of Sambuca, and the arrival of those small glasses, complete with roasted coffee beans floating in the thick sticky liquid amidst a blue flame, was an alchemy that thrilled me for some time.

# 3

## *Which Raffle Did We Win You In?*

A week later I had my first sighting of Thelma. She had her neck in a brace and was wearing a red parachute suit. In fact, over the next few weeks that is all she wore – either in red or black. She had jumped out of an aeroplane for charity, or as she would prefer to say, 'for the hell of it', and injured herself landing awkwardly.

It was during one of my morning envelope-opening sessions that Thelma first put her head round the door of the boardroom and said: 'Hello, darling – which raffle did we win you in?'

Over the next few days she would pop in and stare at me and make odd remarks – none of which I understood. But she was taking more notice of me than I knew. While on switchboard duty one day she asked me to look after her house and her cat – she was going away for the weekend. She put one hand on top of my head and with the other put a bunch of keys in front of me. 'Nik-One will meet you at the house and show you what's what.' I was a bit shocked. She didn't know me at all and who was Nik-One? She insisted the fridge was full and there would be plenty of food. In the event it contained one bottle of vodka, one egg, and a small bowl with a plate resting on top of it, inside which were cold peas and a sausage cut into tiny pieces. The cupboards, however, contained enough cat food to last several months.

Nik-One turned out to be the actor Nikolas

Simmonds. Thelma had been an actress before she became a producer, and they had met at the Open Space Theatre in 1969 when she played Gertrude to his Hamlet. He was one of the most important men in her life. He had won the Most Promising Newcomer Award from *Time Out* in 1971. He would die in 2004 aged only fifty-five after battling with narcolepsy and the depression that accompanied it.

Nik was very good-looking. It was a hot day and he wore a white shirt, dark blue trousers and a pair of old brown lace-up shoes. His beard and moustache were neatly cropped and cut perfectly around his lips, which were full, and gentle as he was. I liked him immediately. He made sure I had his number should anything go wrong – he warned me about the cat, who could be vicious. When he left I wandered around the flat, which seemed very grand to me. There was a large living room with a fireplace at one end, full of exquisitely beautiful furniture. Two sets of tall French windows opened onto a narrow balcony overlooking the tree-lined street. There was a drinks cabinet, which I looked at but never touched. I was terrified of breaking a glass or chipping a decanter. Best of all, there was a record player. Thelma didn't have many records, but the few she had I played continuously. Rachmaninov's Piano Concerto No. 2, Beethoven's Ninth Symphony, and a record of Irish protest songs including 'Take Off the Blood-Stained Bandage'.

My charge, the scary cat Shiva, took to me. She would come and lie on me at night and purr and dribble. I was too frightened to move her; it was apparently not unusual for her to draw blood.

\*

Thelma had short red hair and wicked sparkling eyes framed by heavy spectacles. Her chiselled cheekbones and her thin lips were defining features that endured the passage of time. Thin lips, she maintained, were the preserve of the highly talented. Kenneth Branagh, Laurence Olivier, Zoë Wanamaker – just about anyone we would ever work with who had thin lips was deemed quite brilliant. Thelma was striking, radiant, utterly captivating. She had immense authority coupled with a playfulness, a childlike quality that set her apart from others, who she often referred to as 'the grown-ups'.

Suddenly, turning up at those offices took on a new dimension: I might get to see that mad woman with the red hair, she might come and talk to me again. Her cut-glass accent would deliver a rapid gunfire of instructions, questions and pronouncements. I'd never met anyone who spoke to people as she did. Far from finding the gun-toting, irreverent language she some-times used shocking, I was excited and enthralled by it, believing this was the way truly brilliant and interesting people should speak. One day an unsuspecting young man was waiting for an appointment in the reception area. Thelma was running late and was quizzing Mal-colm about him. The next thing I knew she was shouting through the open door: 'Are you pretty, you cunt? If you are, you can come in now, but if not you had better piss off.' This was followed by her very particular guffaw and the often-repeated comment, 'Oh, darling, I've amused myself.' When I tried this language myself in the outside world, the results were not altogether successful. Only Thelma could turn a word almost universally consid-ered offensive into something that sounded affectionate and funny.

Such was her impatience not to miss important phone calls, or indeed any precious working moment, that she'd regularly come out of the lavatory flashing her magnificent breasts and doing up the endless poppers as she made her way back down the corridor to her office. She was very proud of her breasts, and with good reason. She received a letter from a serious fan of her 'tits', as she always called them, while performing at the Theatre Royal Haymarket in 1967:

PERSONAL LETTER.

Miss Thelma Holt,
Actress,
25, Haymarket,
L o n d o n  SW l.,

Dear Miss Holt,

Best wishes from Finland. It's nicely hot, a fan fare to heat wave I suppose.

I must tell you, that looked just fine on "Z Cars" a part named as Another Fairy Tail, which I saw only yesterday at TV.

This may sounds rather strange, but your bossom looked just great, and because I have had a troubles with my own, I can only adore the woman, that has the bossom alike.

I wonder you were wearing some nice bra? My own bossom is 38 with B. I really like to have a bra like had on that particular act. Will you like to send the bra you wore then to me, if it's still at your wardrobe, no matter if it's a bit shabbied.

This must be the most unusual reguest you have ever had, but you do me very happy if you put it to parcel or a large envelop, please in letter post, if it suits for you. I am delighted to wear that beautiful bra, or just keep it as a souvenier of the woman, who looked so fine in it. Thank you.

I hope you best of luck in your work, as an actress, and I hope to see you again on the TV. I point out that this is not a joke. Thank you.

Thelma's finer features extended to her arms, wrists and feet – all of which were small and delicate. Her 'arse', as she always referred to it, was not in that category. One night in the Roundhouse bar, as Thelma was about to add the tonic, Lady Diana Cooper clasped her wrist with a claw-like hand and said, 'Not with your arse, dear.' She has drunk only neat vodka ever since.

Thelma soon started to summon me to do various things for her – very small things. What I didn't realise was that she was building up to stealing me from the Marketing Department. She did this without my knowledge, I was just suddenly aware that a whole lot of people were not talking to one another and I was soon sitting in Thelma's office perched on a stool with a tiny card table for a desk and an old electric typewriter, almost larger than the table itself, balanced on top.

'Darling, you are going to do the biographies for the programme.' This meant that I was given the handwritten sheets that had been collected from the company by the stage manager and had to type them out in no more than 150 words each. 'Just cut as you see fit, darling, there's a lot of crap in there.' Nobody seemed to be at all concerned that I was not in a position to judge which productions should be cut from a CV and which should remain. But I went on the principle that if I'd heard of it then it stayed and if I hadn't, it went. 'David is married to Cathy and enjoys fishing at weekends' also got the red line through it.

Thelma mischievously phoned John Alderton to tell him that 'the child' was rewriting his biography – it says something for him that he didn't seem bothered and would eventually refer to me as 'Peanut'. He and his actress wife, Pauline Collins, were both founder members of the Theatre of Comedy. A very attractive couple, they had a rather cosy kind of glamour about them and radiated happiness and a degree of normality. I couldn't see either of them arguing about the size of their photographs outside the theatre, or the colour of their dressing room. I had once overheard Thelma on the phone with someone's agent; their client was not happy with either of the aforementioned. I was a little shocked and assumed there was something wrong with the actor involved, a notion Thelma did nothing to disabuse me of.

One evening my brother Hodie was in London before setting off to travel around Europe for six months. We were very close and I was going to miss him. I went to wave him goodbye from Victoria Coach Station, trying not to cry as I watched his face in the window recede through the bright lights of a London night. I ran all the way back to the Shaftesbury Theatre to join Thelma and Malcolm in the bar, my heart pounding with anxiety and sadness, but also with an adrenalised high I'd not experienced before – shock waves of the new life I'd landed in. These characters who until only days ago I had no idea existed. Thelma, Malcolm, Pearl and the painted ladies.

I continued to run errands and work the switchboard, but Thelma would usually find a reason to have me do something else, however small. Frankly, I was happy to do anything other than the switchboard. One day she asked me to make coffee for her and a very glamorous producer from Australia. I delivered it, but minutes later she called me back.

'Come here, darling.' I moved towards her. 'Closer, darling' – and very quickly she put a finger across my face and smudged off some of my freckles. Then, turning to her stunned-looking guest, she said simply, 'There, told you they weren't real.'

That afternoon Thelma asked me to come and see her about my acting aspirations. After training at RADA, she had gone on to have a not entirely unsuccessful career as an actress. However, she maintained that as Maggie Smith and Judi Dench were contemporaries, and as she was never going to be as good as them, she had lost interest. She had decided, when touring a play and putting up with what she considered were appalling terms and conditions for actors, that she could make it all better. And that's why she had become a producer. She advised I follow the same path: 'You would never make a career as an actress and you have a flair for producing.' She then dictated a letter from me to Sir Oliver Neville (who at that time ran RADA) explaining that I would not be attending any audition as I was now working for Thelma Holt. She finished my acting career before it began. It seemed that overnight I was set on another course. As Thelma pointed out when comparing herself with Maggie Smith and Judi Dench, 'If you can't be *that* good then what's the point, darling? – eighty-five per cent unemployed – so far better to be the people employing the top fifteen per cent, darling. No, you must do what I do.'

Having already begun to suspect that the life I'd thought I was destined for since about the age of fourteen was perhaps not for me, my doubts intensified when I accompanied a friend to see an actor she knew in a play at the National Theatre starring Ralph Richardson – in what would turn out to be his last stage appearance. Michael Bryant was a highly skilled leading man who was also happy to play supporting roles – often elevating a mediocre production to another level; he was a major player on and off stage at the National for several decades. After the performance she asked him if he had any advice for a young girl wanting to embark on a career as an actor. He looked at me and said, 'Have you got a skin like a fucking rhinoceros?'

# 4

## *Sight & Sound*

The first proper job Thelma gave me was introduced in the following manner.

I was told to get a notepad and pencil and to go into the boardroom where 'someone' was waiting. This someone would need help. I was to see exactly what she needed and then get on with it, anything I didn't understand I was to ask Thelma. I walked into a smoke-filled room to find Vanessa Redgrave sitting at the end of a long table with her address book, surrounded by a disarray of notebooks and bags. Even sitting down she was tall, and incredibly beautiful – in an unselfconscious way. Her voice was rich, smooth and a little broken, with a particularly seductive rhythm to it. She was putting on a Sunday event at the Lyric Theatre, a one-off performance called *Chekhov's Women and Their Lives*, and she wanted Thelma's help.

Vanessa and Thelma were old friends, and had known each other since the 1950s when Thelma had understudied Vanessa in a production of *A Touch of the Sun*. Thelma was very amusing about the fact that when they had both taken part in the anti-Vietnam War protest outside the American Embassy in 1968, Thelma was left lying in Trafalgar Square alone after Vanessa had been carried away. Nobody knew who Thelma was so they didn't bother with her.

I had seen Vanessa in *Playing for Time* when I

was at school and had been deeply affected by it. But sitting with her in that room, all I could think about was getting it right, whatever it was. Thelma was bigger in my mind than Vanessa. In that respect, I was passing a test and Thelma was delighted to find that I was not star-struck, merely talent-struck. I was nervous, though, and said almost nothing, simply writing down everything Vanessa said. I then went immediately to Malcolm, who pointed me in all the right directions, which meant organising the printing of the flyers, collecting props, making phone calls and generally running around. The difference was that this time there seemed to be a point to it, I wasn't just opening mail or sitting at the switchboard.

Vanessa was easy to be around; she was in her own biosphere and had a relaxed kind of privacy about her that neither invited closeness nor refused accessibility. We would go on to work with her over the course of several years and Vanessa became a regular visitor to our office, often roping us in to help organise benefits for various charitable causes and unwittingly creating much humour along the way.

She once rushed into our office and in a great breathless hurry, lovingly placed a brand-new hardback copy of *Children of the Arbat* by the Soviet author Anatoly Rybakov on each of our desks. She then left. Looking at one another in amusement we opened our books – each copy had been individually dedicated and signed. 'What does this mean?' said Malcolm, suspiciously. A few days later Thelma received a call from Vanessa and once again we were called into action as the quick support group for yet another cause.

*

By the time I sat beside Thelma in the stalls of the Lyric Theatre on Shaftesbury Avenue one Sunday morning to watch a rehearsal of *Chekhov's Women*, I felt the first of many stomach rolls as I watched more real live acting taking place before my eyes. Thelma had also of course been testing me with this exercise. She needed to know how I would conduct myself, not just in terms of the detail of the work itself, but how I would behave when faced with a star, an actor in a dressing room, an angry technician. These skills, she maintained, were unteachable. When this little project was over she told me that I had excellent instincts, that I reminded her of herself in her youth. I felt I had received a passport into an exclusive club. Her approbation meant more than anything and her unselfconscious tutelage had begun.

Shortly after this I was put in an office as an assistant to an American woman named Annie Dorszinski. A febrile, skinny New Yorker with cropped hair, forever drawing on a cigarette, she did everything at high speed and brought a particular kind of alien energy to the organisation. Annie reported to Thelma, but ran her own department that took care of press and marketing.

One of my first jobs was to do a raft of availability requests on actors, older men to take over a very small part and understudy in one of Ray's shows. This entailed searching for the actor's details in *Spotlight* (there are now five or six books for each sex, but in those days there were only two), a call to the actor's agent, an explanation of who we were, what the show was and the dates; they would then tell you if the actor was free and interested. The first three I enquired about were all dead. Even Annie, the seasoned New Yorker, raised an eyebrow when she heard me say for the third time in a row, 'Oh, I'm so terribly sorry to hear that.'

From our office window we had a clear view of the neon signs on the theatre for *Two into One*. Most mornings one or more of the letters would be unlit and it was my job to ring the signage company and report the faulty letters. Sometime during the day men would appear with ladders and replace letters.

London appeared a different colour in those days, even at night, and something always seemed to be broken. In the island between the offices and the theatre in the centre of Shaftesbury Avenue, a collection of drunken men would huddle together clutching tins of Strongbow and Special Brew. I'd never seen anything like this before; Annie told me they were homeless and given shelter at night by a charity nearby. When it was wet and cold they stood hunched like penguins, occasionally lurching towards cars or passers-by, shouting ineffectual expletives. In the hot weather their leathery skin blistered when they fell asleep on the benches, and an acrid smell permeated the area.

The tragedy and comedy masks (the logo for the Theatre of Comedy) decorated the blue door through which one entered from the street, climbing the carpeted stairs to the far more fragrant suite of offices. L'Air du Temps was the perfume of choice for one of the company managers, and that was the perfume I remember smelling when I arrived there for the first time, because for a while my mother wore it.

I helped Annie and learnt a lot. When she was on holiday I ran the department. I took this very seriously, but I was also struck by how easy I found it and how much I enjoyed it. Another of my tasks was to answer letters sent in to Ray Cooney. He used exclamation marks a lot, and I would write short letters in his style. These letters impressed Thelma, who couldn't tell the difference between a genuine Cooney and one of my inventions.

I was also sent to see productions on the fringe that Thelma had been invited to but didn't always have the time to attend. I'd then have to write a short report, the idea being that if it was any good, she would go herself. My first report impressed, only because it made her laugh. She wrote me a memo, at the bottom of which she scrawled in thick black marker: *Learn to type faster or you are no use to me.* Had Malcolm not delivered the memo in person, telling me how pleased with me she was, I'd have been mortified; it did indeed take me an age to type anything.

I was sent for ten consecutive evenings to learn to touch-type. I would leave the offices in the dark and walk round the corner to the Sight & Sound building on Charing Cross Road. The room was very brightly lit and full of old typewriters, the keys of which were covered in grey plastic. We sat in rows, plugged into earphones, typing whatever was spoken to us down the wire: 'The quick brown fox jumped over the lazy dog', etc. Nobody talked to anyone. We were all there for one hour to achieve the best speed possible, then get out. During the day at the office I would force myself to stick to the proper way, however slowly this meant things got typed, and not to revert to my speedier two-finger method. It was a dreary experience but the end result quickly proved to be a valuable and time-saving skill.

\*

Around this time, I realised that I could not afford to keep working for nothing. The money I had saved was running out, and cheap though my accommodation was, I needed to support myself. Neither did I want to stay at the hostel for much longer. Though I had made good friends there and the location was perfect, there were things that were not. I'd been unable to wash clothes on more than one occasion because a woman dressed as a nurse and wearing Marigold rubber gloves had locked herself in the washroom in the basement and was scrubbing everything repeatedly: all the washing machines, tumble dryers, the walls, and finally, if you peered through the slit of glass for long enough, you would see her washing herself.

I bought a copy of *The Stage* and began circling in red anything that I thought I might be able to do. A lot of these jobs were totally inappropriate, but I didn't know that. I had been out on an errand and when I returned Annie told me that Thelma wanted to see me; she also told me that she had seen the paper on my desk and had asked Annie what I was doing. I was summoned and asked, or told, the following:

1. 'How much is the rent in that nuthouse you live in?'
2. 'You don't need much for food, darling, just don't eat.'
3. 'You don't need travel money, darling, you can walk everywhere.'

Thelma then went into the Financial Director's office and told him that the company had exploited the child for months, the child was now an invaluable asset and he needed to find £70 per week to keep the child. This was paid to me in cash and was enough to cover the basics – just. This was my first lesson in Thelma always getting what she wanted.

We celebrated in the bar of the Shaftesbury Theatre, Thelma and Malcolm drinking their miniature bottles of vodka, while I tried to keep up with the red wine. That's another thing I was learning from Thelma: how to drink. Not that I had her cast-iron constitution. The next day I didn't turn up for work. They called the hostel, messages were left in my pigeonhole. Someone was sent to knock on my door. I heard and saw nothing. I eventually woke at 3 p.m. and found the sink in my room full of my clothes, covered in red wine and peanuts, which was all that my stomach contained the night before.

Thelma's final production at the Theatre of Comedy was a Feydeau farce, *Le Dindon*, in an adaptation by John Wells (perhaps most famous for playing Denis Thatcher in *Anyone for Denis?*) which was titled *Women All Over*. She brought Adrian Noble from the RSC to direct it and the cast was led by Eileen Atkins. Adrian was at this time living with the casting director Joyce Nettles, and so with them came an impressive cast and for me the first sight of a 'real' director. This meant someone dressed in crumpled linen shirts and jackets, jeans and sandals, rather than pale blue trousers with a crease down the front and V-neck sweaters in bright yellow with pale blue diamonds on them and soft cream shoes. Adrian and Ray Cooney were different species. Adrian would pace up and down the office discussing the play and throwing out names, while tugging at the one or two hairs that seemed to sprout from his otherwise smooth face. Ray always looked as if he was off to play a round of golf.

*Women All Over* was destined for the Edinburgh Festival and then to Bromley, supposedly en route to the West End. Thelma made me responsible for getting the creative team to Edinburgh and liaising with the people who handled all the press. Under Annie's instruction I dealt with photographers, with the marketing and advertising team, and began to learn just how much scaffolding there was behind a production. No doubt I asked Malcolm many more questions than I can remember and the illusion that I was doing all this alone was cleverly manufactured by Thelma, giving me free rein on carefully selected tasks, but of course my safety net was a big one.

Thelma took me pretty much everywhere with her, and this was how I learnt the ropes. I would accompany her on visits to actors' dressing rooms, where I'd rarely speak – unless spoken to – and got used to being with her all day and occasionally evenings, often until very late. She took me to Bromley one night to see the opening performance of *Women All Over*, and on the train back to London Eileen Atkins and the cast drank champagne with us out of paper cups and there was laughter about my freckles. Thelma still told everyone about this and would continue to rub them off when she felt so inclined, to prove they weren't real. Shortly after that I stopped applying them. I didn't have time any more.

I later learnt that however convivial a family feeling the business seemed to engender, I would need to be on my guard.

'The child, darling. Hands off!' was what Thelma said as she placed her hand on the knee of the first man to molest me. While on tour she had engineered to sit next to him on the plane after she had got wind of the incident.

I was woefully unprepared to sense any threat or deal with such things myself. I knew that men raped and murdered women, but I had no idea that they would casually help themselves to parts of your body, or jump on you and stick their tongues down your throat while you were going about your daily business. In the early years, before I became confident and wise enough to disallow even the opportunity, there were an uncomfortable number of incidents.

The most bizarre of these took place one day when I was alone in the office. Thelma was in a meeting, and Malcolm had temporarily disappeared. I was on the phone, having a fairly intense conversation with an agent about dates and various actors' availabilities, when in wandered a world-famous actor. I smiled at him, acknowledging his presence. I knew he was expected, so was sure Malcolm would appear at any moment to summon Thelma from her meeting. Suddenly, I became aware that he was no longer in my field of vision. At that moment, Thelma emerged and began talking to the aforementioned world-famous actor's wife outside our office door.

The agent on the phone was now in full flow. Without warning, a hand was plunged into the top of my shirt and secured itself around my right breast. I was so stunned that I continued talking to the agent as if nothing was happening. At the same time, I wondered what the agent would think if I said, 'I have to go now because X is cupping my right breast with his hand.' She would no doubt have thought I was delusional. The hand remained in position, the actor's wife still hovering outside the door talking to Thelma, until Malcolm reappeared, at which point X removed his hand from my breast. I concluded my conversation with the agent.

Thelma and Malcolm appeared back in their chairs and she asked me for the list of availabilities. 'You'll never guess what just happened,' I said. Thelma's mouth rarely opened in silence. But it did, that day.

# 5

## *In Limbo*

In 1985 Thelma was invited by Peter Hall to join him at the National Theatre to run the department responsible for regional and international touring and West End transfers. This was a blow for me, I was to be left behind. At her farewell party, Thelma asked me in front of everyone, 'Well, darling, do you want to come and work at the National Theatre?' I shrugged casually, believing this to be nothing more than words. Thelma laughed – 'Look at the child, shrugging at the idea of the bloody NT!' I was on the verge of tears because the thought of life without Thelma was grim.

She promised to take me out for supper now and then, a promise she kept. This would usually be a little restaurant on Shaftesbury Avenue called Il Pasetto. It was here that she first taught me to forge her signature – to sign her credit card slips. This skill, once perfected, was sampled on letters, charge card slips and even on occasion, cheques. She found it very amusing. The practice, however, was cut short when a horrified friend informed me it was in fact a crime.

Sometimes we'd go to The Ivy (I had no idea The Ivy was anywhere special), always ordering the same: an avocado starter, followed by fishcakes – which we would share – Thelma telling the waiter, 'One fishcake and two plates please, darling – the child doesn't eat.' (This habit would go on well into my thirties, to the dismay of fellow diners. 'I can recommend the Dover sole,' Diana Rigg said one evening in Sheekey's as the waiter hovered. 'We'll share the fishcakes, darling. We can't eat more than one,' said Thelma.)

On these evenings out she would tell me about life at the National and ask me what was happening at the Theatre of Comedy. What was happening for me was nothing. I felt myself sliding into a void. I had become a Cinderella figure. Having done all those exciting things, I was now back on the switchboard and typing out letters for the Finance Director. Letters which I would get wrong most of the time, so his secretary would hand them back to me with any tiny mistake covered in highlighter pen, thus making the use of Tipp-Ex impossible so the whole thing would have to be done again. I missed Thelma and Malcolm, and their new world seemed a far-off place, seen only in glimpses. Thelma had also inherited a third team member, a woman who had been doing the job for some time. So the notion that I might ever join them seemed impossible.

When Thelma and Malcolm left the offices, I had felt all the excitement of the job disappear. There was no dynamism or urgency and little sense that we were working in theatre production. I had in a short space of time been stamped with the Thelma seal of approval. Now she had moved on I was tolerated, but certainly not worth even £70 a week to anyone else there. Thelma had gone, and taken my freckles with her. She had also left me with a new name. It had been 'darling' to start with, and then 'the child'. But very quickly she had decided I was to be called Sweetpea. She said I reminded her of the flower, but she also thought I was like the baby Popeye took to the races who picked out the winning horses. She said I had good instincts, and what she called 'a built-in shit detector'.

I went to Dorset for the weekend to stay with my parents and seriously considered doing something entirely different, possibly even going abroad for a while. But I didn't want to do anything else, even though Hodie's recent travels had made him suddenly far more worldly than I was. I had fallen under the spell of the theatre, or more specifically, Thelma's world of the theatre. Just walking into an auditorium set my heart thumping, let loose the butterflies in my stomach. But I had no money, no university degree, and it seemed my mentor had abandoned me.

We had been for a long walk and on returning in the late afternoon I found a message on the answer machine from Thelma. It simply said: 'Hello, Mrs Slight, it's Thelma Holt and I am trying to track Sweetpea down rather urgently. Would you ask her to call me.' I thought she wanted me to look after her house, as I knew she was off on tour again shortly. When I reached her on Saturday night, she said, 'Get your arse back to London on the first train you can tomorrow. You start at the National on Monday morning.' In the next breath she told me, 'You'll get tuppence halfpenny – everyone wanted the job and nobody wanted you, darling, but you'll be fine.'

# 6

## *Going National*

I was terrified and didn't sleep for days. I'd get up at
5 a.m. each morning with appalling butterflies in
my stomach and, unable to eat breakfast, would arrive
hours early at the National Theatre stage door. I worried that Thelma had made a terrible mistake; perhaps
I wasn't as clever as she thought, and certainly would
not be up to the job. Actually, I had no idea what the job
entailed. All she had told me was that the woman in the
post was thirty-five and was having a nervous breakdown. I knew of course that she wasn't; that this was a
figure of speech and perhaps Thelma's way of signalling
to me the colossal nature of the workload. I did wonder,
though, if my predecessor wanted to leave before there
was any danger of Thelma driving her to one.

Thankfully, Thelma didn't tell me until later that
she'd met some considerable resistance from senior
management at the National on account of my age and
the fact that my CV was non-existent. No, Thelma had
replied loftily, you could fit her CV on a postage stamp.
Further protestations arose when Thelma gave them
my name. The head of the Press Department at the time
had baulked and said she couldn't possibly call anyone
Sweetpea. A defiant Thelma replied, 'Well, you can call
her what you like, and she will probably smile at you,
she has a nice smile. But she won't respond to anything
other than Sweetpea.' All of which did very little for my

reputation. My worry was that if a thirty-five-year-old woman found it stressful, how on earth was I going to cope? The worst thing of all being that Thelma wouldn't be there for the first three days. She was out on the regional part of the tour for *Animal Farm*, before it went overseas. Thank God Malcolm was around for vital support, although it was still all relatively new to him too.

I was to have two weeks' induction with the previous incumbent, followed by a two-week probationary period. My job on Thelma's team meant that I was responsible for making sure that the actors, the creative team, stage managers and technicians all reached their tour destination, whether in this country or abroad. Doing deals with travel agents to find the cheapest and best routes, applying for visas and passports, planning itineraries, working with the tour managers with regards to transporting the sets and costumes – these were all part of my job description. It was all about detail and liaising with almost every department at the NT. This sounds simple now, but then it appeared hugely daunting, if only due to the sheer numbers involved.

The woman from whom I was taking over turned out to be rather lovely and she was patient and thorough in her hand-over. All this was in the days before email, so different parts of the world required different means of communication. For example, fax covered most places but not Russia; there we had to rely on telex, and in some instances, telegram. Most of the women around me seemed so much older; they were of course all very young – most in their late twenties or early to mid-thirties. But to a nineteen-year-old, they were very grown up indeed. However pleasant they were, I felt a certain coolness.

I continued to turn up early for the next two days, at least an hour before any of the offices, or indeed the canteen, were open. On day three, Linda on stage door took me to one side and advised me to come closer to ten than eight or nine. I was counting rail tickets out when Thelma walked in and found me at my desk. I can still remember the way she smiled at me. She told me later how proud she was of me, and I was just glad that I had managed to get through almost the first week without incident.

Our offices adjoined Casting, presided over by the formidable Gillian Diamond. Her glamorous assistant Penny and I sat opposite one another in an office shared by both departments, with Thelma behind me, visible through a hatch in the wall, and Gillian behind Penny. These two departments were a very busy hub of activity as actors were always coming to visit one or another, with stage management and crew members streaming in and out on a daily basis.

It took me weeks to learn who everyone was. Unable to tell the difference between the armourer and Michael Bryant, I would have entire conversations with various people and once they had left I would ask Penny who they were. I made her laugh a lot – not intentionally, but I think she found my way of coping genuinely comical.

I knew who Peter Hall was, even before Thelma introduced us, because he'd been pointed out to me. He usually wore black, Nehru-collar shirts and jackets, and smoked fat cigars. He was a big man, not fat but tall and rather like a bulldog, with a large head and sloping shoulders. Bearded, his hair slicked back with some kind of pomade, he resembled a James Bond villain – Dr No came to mind. Peter's voice was both gentle and emphatic. He seemed always to be calm and measured, despite what I only realised later was a stressful existence. He worked incredibly hard – Thelma always joked that he had a lot of wives to keep.

Learning my way around the building was an achievement in itself. The corridors backstage all looked the same. I discovered how easy it was to get lost when I passed Zoë Wanamaker's dressing room for the third time. The canteen was an exciting but sometimes frightening place to go. It was full of actors, directors, technicians and administrative staff. It was where we all ate breakfast, lunch and supper while working in the building. One would see famous names sharing tables with the backstage crew. Most surprising was the way that these actors would come and join you and chat. I couldn't believe it. I was having breakfast with Anthony Hopkins, lunch with Michael Gambon and supper with Ian McKellen. I soon learnt the canteen was often the best place to nag actors to remember to complete their visa forms, or get their passport photographs taken.

The Green Room was next door. This was the bar strictly for use by members of the company. We could bring guests there after shows in the evening, but it was not open to the public. Sometimes an actor in full costume would be sipping half a pint of Guinness while I ordered vodka for Thelma and a glass of wine for myself. The tannoy would carry the voices of stage managers all round the building: '*King Lear* company, this is your five-minute call, five minutes please.' Or Linda on the stage door asking someone to report in, or alerting someone that their taxi had arrived. One could spend too long there after a hard day's work; there was always someone interesting to talk to and Thelma's 'One for the road, darling' would often turn into three for the road, making it a very long day indeed.

A short journey through the maze of corridors took you down to the back of the Lyttelton or Olivier stages, where we'd pass actors standing in the wings, 'in character', before we passed through a security door to the front-of-house, into the buzz of the theatre foyer and expectant audiences. We would often head for the Hospitality Room (renamed the 'Hostility Room'), used to entertain important guests. To be so proximate to the rehearsal rooms and the actors, to Wardrobe, the props, the wigs, the scenery building, to feel productions being made and rehearsed, all in one building, was a new and all-consuming world to me. A walk down two flights of stairs from our office to the canteen would take me from the frenzied sound of typewriters and hectic phone conversations, to follow in the wake of Peter Hall's cigar smoke as he made his way to a rehearsal room. As the door opened and closed behind him, you could hear sounds of declaiming actors.

With a salary as small as mine it was a considerable perk to be able to see plays for free, or at very reduced rates, and the National was a vast playground with three auditoria. I'd save up to see things outside the NT as well, but the ruins of my memory have shrunk this cornucopia to a few scattered images – *Man to Man* at the Royal Court, with Tilda Swinton in a pair of Y-fronts and what looked like a sock shoved down them, a beautifully lit set of steps in Adrian Noble's production of *Macbeth*, and Mark Rylance's eyelashes the first time I saw him on stage in the Lyttelton Theatre in Mike Alfreds's production of *The Wandering Jew*.

Often when one tour was starting on the road, another one was in the planning stage, so the workload was phenomenal. My first big foreign tour was with Peter Hall's production of *Animal Farm*. The actors played the animals as well as the humans. This was the first production I saw after beginning work at the National and it was the first time I'd seen a book come to life on stage. I was lost in it, totally transported to this other world and incredibly moved by the actors' portrayals of the animals. Thelma would march into the office half-singing, half-speaking, 'Four legs good, two legs bad!' and 'There's no such place as Sugarcandy Mountain, Sugarcandy Mountain is a LIE, LIE, LIE!' In more contemplative moments, she'd give us her own sad little rendition of Boxer the horse's farewell song:

> *'I will be well, friends,*
> *And I'll retire, friends, to the shadow of the chestnut*
>   *tree*
> *With time for thinking*
> *And time for learning*
> *The remainder of my* [pause] *A* [dramatic pause] *B*
> [even more dramatic pause] *C.'*

The entire company was due to fly out of Heathrow and I had been meticulous about letting everyone know the details, on paper and by telephone. A coach would depart from the stage door, but some who lived further out would make their own way to the airport. I would stay near the phone until check-in time had been and gone so that any last-minute problems could be dealt with. I was sitting in the canteen alone one morning with a cup of tea, relieved that the company were now finally on their way, when I saw Gillian Diamond enter the canteen and speak to someone sotto voce. My stomach turned over; I don't know why, but I knew she was trying to find me. She moved towards me without any urgency, put her hand on my shoulder and en route to the coffee machine simply said, 'You had better get back upstairs, child, one of your chickens is at Gatwick.'

Thelma had returned from Zurich, the first venue, and was spending a few days with us before flying out to the next destination. As soon as I heard her opening words – 'Sit down, darling. Now, the armourer . . .' – my heart sank. Because there were guns in the production, the touring company included an armourer who had to travel independently because firearms were not allowed on flights. Arranging transfers for him from one country to another had taken a lot of time and caused me considerable anxiety.

My first thought was that I must have made a mistake with the paperwork and now the armourer was stuck at some border and the guns impounded. I started to explain why I had not completed the last part of his journey, as this was the only thing I thought she might have to be unhappy about. She interrupted me, waving her hands in a dismissive manner: 'Darling, he's dead. They found him in the hotel room this morning – and now someone has stolen all the guns.'

I was shocked, how terrible. This nice man who I had handed tickets to only days earlier, dead in some hotel room in Zurich. It seemed awful. Thelma was unfazed. 'Now, darling, we are going to need to move quickly,

Rosie is calling back in a minute, and we have to get another armourer out there fast.'

Rosie Beattie was the Company Manager and therefore in charge of all the stage management teams. She was often out on tour and would in the future become my primary point of contact regarding most things to do with the company leaving the building, and with foreign companies visiting. Tall and very slender, with short neat hair, Rosie was always dressed in a blouse or sweater and a skirt – never trousers – with stockings and neat shoes. She smoked quite heavily and had a healthy laugh. Strangely, she never smelt of cigarettes. I didn't think she looked like someone who worked in the theatre; she could just as easily have been a headmistress, or the manager of a smart department store. I liked her the moment I met her, she was kind and didn't seem to think it at all odd that I should be doing this job. She was meticulous, incredibly patient, and she loved Thelma and her 'hands-on' way of working.

Stress – and her job was considerably stressful – never defeated Rosie. She would laugh most things off or shake her head with disbelief as she lit yet another cigarette. Even before I got to know her well, I understood that Rosie's particularly reassuring presence and utterly authentic personality would ensure that any situation that unfolded would be kept under control. She did not relish 'drama'.

I, meanwhile, went back to my desk reeling and began to frantically set about finding a new armourer at short notice.

If I thought *this* was shocking, only days later an incident occurred back in London which required Thelma's help. Various people in the building soon learnt that

Thelma's unique way of dealing with things was an incredible new asset. A male member of the company had climbed on top of another and had what he thought was consenting sex, only to be accused the following morning of assault. Thelma asked to see the perpetrator and the accuser, one at a time, so she could get each man's version of events. She saw the accused first; he was over six feet tall and of big build. When the door opened and his accuser walked in, she saw that he was very small and very camp. Having heard both sides, Thelma sat them down together and said, 'If either of you had been to a boarding school, none of this would have been necessary.' Meanwhile, arrangements were being made for the body of the armourer to be flown back to Heathrow, where his widow would collect it. When Thelma arrived back in the office, she said, 'We're in a fucking Joe Orton play, darlings.'

When my induction and probationary period was over, Thelma sent a glittering report to Peter's Head of Finance and I became official. Shortly afterwards, Penny told me plainly that when I had arrived none of them had been keen to take me on board. They were all fond of their former colleague and, frankly, they didn't think I was going to be up to it. But now she said she took her hat off to me; in a short space of time I had won acceptance, having taken to the job 'like a duck to water'.

My salary was minuscule. Thelma took me home one evening and had what would in the future become a customary clear-out of her wardrobe. I was sent home with two large bin liners full of clothes. The result was an interesting mix of the occasional expensive item that I combined with my high-street purchases. Despite the considerable difference in our heights, I think I got away with most of it.

I'd been with Thelma a year and life was becoming complicated, using both the name I'd been christened with and the one Thelma had given me. I would forget which I'd used. At work I was called Sweetpea, and some of my friends too had started to call me by this name. My family, however, and everyone else from my past, continued to refer to me as Jane. But this new world I inhabited had begun with a new name and everyone became used to it. Apparently it would cost £90 to change it on my birth certificate, but as long as I altered my passport, bank account and driving licence (not that I had one), it would be official.

Worrying a little about whether Mum and Dad would be upset about this and wondering how best to broach the matter, the problem was taken out of my hands when Thelma gave an interview to a national newspaper. It was here that my parents first read a reference to me as Sweetpea. My mother rang me to ask if it was true, as she needed to know for the will. I needn't have fretted, because as it happened neither of my parents was bothered, or so they said.

They were just back from a trip to London for a friend's private view. Dad had forgotten to pack any shoes and arrived in town wearing his bright yellow wellingtons with steel toecaps, which he had cut down himself into clog-type affairs with uneven edges. He insisted he could wear these with the black suit and told Mum not to be so 'fucking bourgeois'. She refused to go unless he put on some proper footwear. Mum spent the afternoon trying to find a reasonably priced pair of plain black shoes, ending up in Marks & Spencer, where she purchased a pair he still has to this day; we call them his policeman's shoes. To cap it all, when Mum was packing away the yellow cut-off wellies she noticed something inside and upon investigating found it to be a squashed frog. It was perfectly flat. Neither of us could believe Dad had spent the whole day in these without noticing.

I didn't tell anyone at the theatre about this.

# 7

## Westbourne Terrace

The opportunity to leave the hostel presented itself with remarkable ease. A friend from school who had secured a place at Saint Martins had made friends with a girl called Harriet, who went by Harry and rented a room in an enormous flat in Westbourne Terrace with three other people. One of the flatmates was going travelling for the summer and so they needed to rent her room out for a couple of months. I don't know what I thought would happen after the two months were up, but desperate to leave the confines of the hostel, I took the room.

Mine was the smallest, but only in comparison to the other, ballroom-sized, rooms. We all had balconies, parquet floors and old-fashioned French doors or tall windows that opened either on to Westbourne Terrace, or out on to the back overlooking other balconies and roof terraces. The building had a faded, decadent beauty. Harry and her friends lived on two floors – the first and second. We weren't quite sure who lived on the ground floor; it was empty, but was looked after by the couple who lived in the basement. They once showed us the ground-floor flat – I'd never seen anything like it. There was an actual ballroom; small compared to many, but nevertheless a ballroom. A time capsule untouched and unlived in.

Besides Harry, there was Mark, who looked like a

young Sam Shepard, studying graphic design; Felicity – who fancied Mark; and Polly, who worked for Christie's. They were all lovely and welcomed me into their circle. When I got home from work someone was usually cooking something and we generally all mucked in. It was a very sociable set-up.

Polly was a grown-up, the only one of us who wore suits and came home with a briefcase, which she would toss aside on her way to the fridge saying, 'I need a fucking G&T.' She'd wander around in heels, ice clinking in her glass, while we drank cheap wine and tins of Bavarian lager from Budgens. She always had a boyfriend, who was also grown-up and wore suits. They would go out for nice dinners or disappear to the bedroom for the evening, while we sat around eating jacket potatoes and salad. It felt luxurious, being in a large ramshackle flat, and even sharing facilities was a novelty for me after the hostel. However lucky I'd been there, I had no plans to return.

A wide and gently curved stone stairway led to Harry's room, then continued for two more levels before metamorphosing into a steeper, narrower set of carpeted stairs leading to a door on the fourth floor. It appeared that this flat was empty. I peered through the letterbox and could make out only a very large main room stacked high with furniture. It was still and quiet, and a little eerie. I decided there and then that this was exactly where I was going when Harry's flatmate returned. I went to visit the landlord. Mr Gold was like something out of a Dickens novel. Several layers of overcoats and a dowager's hump, shuffling around in an office that made our facilities at the National look like NASA headquarters. He confirmed that the flat was currently vacant, but didn't seem to want to commit to whether or not he would consider renting it to me.

I rang the following week and begged him to let me have it. He was very interested in the fact that I worked at the National Theatre, and this may have swung it for me. A company let was required to secure it – I had no idea what this was. Thelma sent me to see her accountant and I bought a company off the shelf for £100. Hodie became company secretary, while I committed to file annual company accounts. I then had to find £1,200 in cash as a deposit (rather a lot to someone who was earning £4,800 per year). My bank manager agreed to give me a loan, which I promised to pay back in a month's time when I had secured some flatmates.

During the short gap between moving out of the flat downstairs and securing the top-floor flat, I lived in Thelma's spare room with boxes of my belongings piled high. When at last Mr Gold called to tell me he was satisfied with my paperwork, I took a taxi to an office in deepest North London and collected a huge bunch of keys on a hoop. I had taken the flat unseen, fairly confident that, although on the top floor, the proportions would still be impressive.

My gamble paid off. There were five bedrooms, a large dining area, a separate sitting room, and a big kitchen. The rooms were crammed with 1970s furniture and old television sets, none of which worked. Most impressive, and useful, was the huge dining table, which could easily seat twelve people when wound out with an old turning handle and the third leaf inserted. I discovered a further secret room concealed behind a door, with an old wooden ladder-like staircase up to the loft, which housed the water tanks. This room proved large enough to store all the unwanted furniture.

There was an enormous fridge in the kitchen full of green mould, but it worked. I went to John Lewis and bought a hoover and spent the first weekend cleaning. Hodie had two weeks' work experience with an art director on commercials, so he took one of the rooms temporarily. His first girlfriend from school, who had just secured a place at art school, moved in with her new boyfriend. The finance was in place for at least the first month.

The hostel was already a distant memory, but I missed Scarlett and Nina. Scarlett had gone home to Lancashire, but Nina was still training as a dentist so I invited her for supper, eager to show her my new home. This was a special occasion, and demanded something more festive than jacket potatoes or pasta. So for the first time ever I bought a chicken.

A bird phobia had afflicted me since childhood, triggered by a number of strange incidents. The first of these was when my mother asked me to collect fallen apples from the roof of the chicken house. Being too small to see, I had to stretch my arm up to retrieve the apples and hand them down to my brother, standing below with a basket. Among the apples I felt something warm and soft, which I blindly fumbled with. Using a nearby ladder, we discovered this to be a dead duck.

The trauma of handling this recently deceased bird grew like Topsy. To make matters worse, only days later I was attacked by the family favourite, a hen called Gertie. She got her neck stuck in a feeder and I froze, convinced that if I lifted the lid to free her, she would emerge with a flat, folded neck. While I cried, Hodie removed the lid and the hen promptly flew at me.

Finally, while having tea with a neighbouring farmer and his wife, I witnessed a recently dispatched cockerel carried in by the feet and plonked unceremoniously on the scales, at which point it regained consciousness and started flapping madly. I screamed. His wife told him to finish the bird off properly. He returned moments later and placed it back on the scales. Once again it squawked and flapped about hysterically (as did I) before clambering off the scales and into the pile of scones we had been enjoying.

By the time I moved to London the farmyard nightmare was replaced by the horror that is the urban pigeon. Trafalgar Square had to be avoided at all costs and for many years I was incapable of preparing raw chicken.

In order to buy the chicken I had to pick it up very quickly from the supermarket shelf and throw it into the trolley. Handling them, even in packaging, was fraught with fear, and so reaching checkout was another sweat-inducing moment. By the time I got it home, I had an hour and a half before Nina was due to arrive. I was sure I could do it. Having succeeded in getting it out of the plastic wrapping, I'd then had to remove the neck and giblets. I managed this by holding the bird in place with a scrunched up tea-towel and then used a fork to pull out the bits without having to touch them. I went to rinse it under the cold water tap but while doing this imagined the horror of it coming to life and promptly dropped it in the sink. There it remained, like some alien that would at any moment slide up and out of the sink, hit the floor with a fleshy thud and then shoot across the room and attach itself to my face.

I ran from the kitchen. The door remained closed until Nina arrived, at which point she retrieved the chicken from the sink. We ate very late.

# 8

## A Beginner's Guide to Thelma

Alan Rickman says I'm a pussycat if you stroke me the right way. I'm intolerant of fools but I'm very soft on talent. Mediocrity loathes talent and women are better at loathing and loving than men. I've been disliked intensely by people suffering from delusions of adequacy – they don't like being around me, but I prefer the company of my betters.

Thelma Holt

On leaving the Roundhouse late one night, Thelma saw a large brand-new white caravan parked outside. It gleamed in the moonlight. She removed a stick of Dior No. 21 lipstick from her bag and scrawled down the side of it *'Get your caravan off my land you cunt.'* The following morning Rowan Atkinson arrived at her office with a large bunch of flowers and a bottle of vodka apologising, but explaining that he had in fact paid rent for the caravan to Thelma's head of security. Thelma thanked him for the flowers and vodka but asked where the replacement for her stick of Dior No. 21 lipstick was.

Watching television with a friend one evening, she failed to recognise her second husband. 'Who's that good-looking actor?' she asked. Her friend replied, 'Are you joking? – you were married to him!'

Unable to master instructions for the dishwasher,

she has stored wine in it for the past thirty years.

She maintains that she killed her twin brother in the womb – 'There wasn't room for both of us, darling' – and made an effigy of her sister, which she buried in a shoebox at the end of the garden.

Her husband Patrick was Danish and once when making a classic Danish dish called *frikadeller* for their dinner guests, she found herself without the crucial ingredient – oatmeal or breadcrumbs. Finding some walnuts, but without a suitable implement with which to mash them, she chewed and spat them into the bowl.

We had a meeting one evening at her house with Alan Rickman and various others. She and I were laying out sandwiches from M&S on platters and setting them on the dining room table. Just before the guests were due to arrive I discovered one of the cats curled up on the egg mayonnaise arrangement. Thelma picked her up, turned the sandwiches over, blew on them, and said to me, 'Don't eat these ones, darling.'

Thelma's ability to make things happen against almost any odds was her greatest skill. How she got there might sometimes make her seem, to those who didn't know her, difficult, scary, even unlikeable. The more impossible the task, the more determined she was that it should happen.

She adored me, that much was clear, but it didn't stop her being incredibly tough. I challenged her on this one night over a curry in Westbourne Grove. We did a lot of our pathologising this way. I accused her of being hard on me in a manner she never was with Malcolm. There were days when he irritated her and days when I irritated her. Except I know I got the sharper side of her tongue. 'You're absolutely right – I know I'm being unfair and irrational but I do expect much more of women, I really do. What's a female misogynist? – because I am one.'

There are far more women in the top jobs in theatre nowadays than there were thirty years ago, but the Royal Shakespeare Company and the National Theatre have only ever been run by men. When Thelma remortgaged her house to finance the first production of Thelma Holt Ltd in 1990, she was the only high-ranking female producer in London. As a 'devious Jesuitical creature' – her own description of herself – the question of feminism was not an issue; for her, the means justified the end. She wished to be recognised for what she did, not for what she did *as a woman*.

A personal life seemed very much a secondary consideration as far as Thelma was concerned. She had one of course (after all, she did manage three husbands), but work was a priority and she expected a similar commitment from us. In the beginning I relished this degree of involvement, although I did exhaust myself trying to remain popular with my friends outside the business, or relied on their goodwill if I didn't see them for weeks on end. A love life was even trickier. For Thelma, her life in the theatre *was* her life. She didn't see this as any kind of sacrifice, it was a choice. Her ways of relaxing outside, which were rare, more often than not didn't involve other people. She liked nothing better than an empty morning in which to sit in her enormous bed with a stack of newspapers and the television news, followed by a wander round an antiques market.

She said that I stopped her being lonely. What I did was to get her occasionally to go home – I could always tell when she was over-tired to a crippling degree and nothing good would come of it. Thelma wasn't short of companions, if she wanted to she could dine with someone different every night of the week. But on the whole, if she's not able to sit and talk about her work, she very quickly becomes bored. One evening I left her sitting in the bar at the theatre; I was dead on my feet and Thelma's unstoppable energy could be relentless. I dropped in on Jeremy, our Company Manager, backstage to say I was leaving and perhaps he might join her if he had time. He told me he would – but, 'Frankly, Sweetpea, she'd be happy to talk to a swing bin if it would listen.'

Thelma's great skill, talking, usually got us out of trouble, but on rare occasions it achieved the opposite effect. After we produced *Macbeth*, she said that her mistake had been in hiring the young director on the basis that he had agreed with everything she said about the play. She confessed to having talked non-stop during their meeting and only realised, with the accuracy of hindsight, that he had said nothing interesting about the play at all. The irony here was that the play was dear to her heart, and we had already cast Rufus Sewell in the title role.

When in the autumn of 1990 she brought a Chinese version of the same play to the National, a brief programme note was her only concession to any kind of translation, and no surtitles were available. She didn't want them to interfere with the truly acrobatic nature of the production. The extraordinary back flips, triple somersaults and dives through the air were so commented upon that it was decided that we would feature them in a special NT Platform. These were discussions or interviews that took place in the theatre earlier in the evening, before the main performance.

Despite our excitement, the Platform was looking decidedly empty – no tickets had been sold. 'Right, Pealet,' she said, having put the phone down on the box office once more. 'We need bums on seats – follow me.' We went down to the box office and Thelma asked them to print out a hundred tickets. She gave me half and we went outside on to the South Bank. 'You go that way,' she said, pointing to the right, 'and I'll go this way. Don't come back until you have fifty people. And get a move on, we go up in an hour.'

I'd given away half the tickets when I looked to my left to see if I could spot Thelma. She looked mad, shouting 'National Theatre! – free tickets!' and waving handfuls of tickets in the air. 'Right,' she said, pushing her glasses up her nose, 'get up to the Green Room and the canteen and collect anybody you can find, darling.'

As Thelma and I stood at the back of the stalls before taking our seats, she leant towards me and said, 'Perfectly respectable, darling' – something she always said when there was just enough of an audience to avoid pain for those on stage.

Thelma could drive Malcolm and me to the edges of exhaustion and exasperation, to the point of wanting – as he often said – to bury an axe in the back of her skull. Equally, she could make you get out of bed in the morning simply dying to get to the office. Thelma had a finite boredom threshold, so if we were very busy and she had no one to torture on the phone, she would interfere with one or both of us. Usually this resulted in Malcolm holding up both hands from the keyboard and saying, 'How many hands do you see!' and in my case ignoring her completely. 'What's wrong with her?' she'd ask Malcolm when repeatedly unable to attract my attention with the constant repetition of 'Pea', 'Pea', 'Pea!' ... pause ... 'cunt'. 'You!' he'd reply.

Eventually, getting no joy from either of us, she would go and buy us something for tea. Thelma and I would share a packet of Reese's Peanut Butter Cups, and Malcolm would have a Rice Krispies bar. On her return, she'd often announce, 'Darlings ... I've had an idea ...' This we dreaded. There was no such thing as a lunch break. 'What's that?' I used to ask friends. We had fifteen minutes, half an hour if we were lucky, eating something at the desk and still 'talking shop' as she called it. Sometimes, when very stressed, she and I would get silly and throw chairs around the office, or scream. We'd often get quite hysterical. This drove Malcolm mad and he would either send us away into another room or insist on silence.

Our office walls were covered in production photographs: Robert Maxwell (this came down later), one of me as a baby, Thelma as a Sixties pin-up, photos of our favourite actors or from current productions, awards and posters from our various plays. They were also covered in quotations. These we collected, but mostly they were Thelma's own words, things she said which amused us and which I would record and then blow up large. 'Theatre is for wankers' (when someone pissed her off); 'Mediocrity rises' (when someone she thought without talent got a powerful position); 'I've had this before with Bath, they never answer their phones' (when she was unable to raise either the company manager or the box office at Bath Theatre Royal); 'There is no room in the theatre for pessimists' (when someone told her something was not possible).

Thelma was never one for political correctness, she said whatever she wanted. She once came back from a meeting at the Arts Council (where someone once described her thus: in 'very shabby clothes with her begging bowl') and said, 'Darlings, if there was something wrong with me they'd have given us the money!'

When particularly bored, she would meddle. Peter Hall once said that if there wasn't a problem for Thelma to solve, she would create one, just so she could solve it. When Peter's production of Tennessee Williams's *Orpheus Descending* was in technical rehearsals in Bath, prior to the London transfer, a call came from Thelma at the Hilton Hotel demanding that one of us come down immediately with a notebook. Malcolm was busy, so I went.

There had been some discrepancy between the designer's notion and an authenticity that Vanessa Redgrave was insisting on regarding the famous snakeskin jacket worn by the character Val. To this end, Vanessa had filled a bath with water and was soaking the leather and snakeskin off old shoes picked up from charity shops. These scraps she was intending to stitch onto an old woollen cardigan. This was her idea of the famous snakeskin jacket, the official version of which was being made as per the designer's instructions. Thelma didn't like the designer. Vanessa and Thelma sat in the hotel room throwing out ideas and I made notes from my position propped up on the bed.

This kind of meddling would sometimes produce interesting results, but could equally prove to be a big waste of everyone's time. But her love of actors meant she'd do almost anything to make them happy, and that was a very happy company.

Every night of the week, one or all of us would visit the actors before the performance and at least twice a week watch the production, often followed by a get-together of some sort. On one occasion Miriam Margolyes made salt beef sandwiches with pickles for the entire company. Miriam was sharing a dressing room with two other actresses and I put my head in one evening to find one of them lighting joss sticks. 'What a lovely smell,' I said. She looked at me over her glasses. 'Yes, well, it's rather necessary,' she said, gesturing towards Miriam's empty chair. 'Oh, why?' I asked innocently. 'She farts for England,' she said, in a whisper and without a hint of malice.

I loved this play and the poetry of Tennessee Williams's language. I'd seen the film version, *The Fugitive Kind*, as a teenager, starring Marlon Brando as Val and Anna Magnani as Lady. The play was in the first volume of drama I bought from Foyles bookshop on Charing Cross Road. I wanted to read for myself Val's description of the bird without legs who can't ever land so has to stay its whole life on the wing.

Even though Vanessa wasn't matched in stature by her leading man, the quality of the supporting actors and Peter's staging meant all the horror and the sadness in the play was up there on stage at the Theatre Royal Haymarket. I would emerge from the stage door with the moving final words of Carol Cutrere ringing in my ears as I made my way across Trafalgar Square towards Charing Cross Tube station:

*Wild things leave skins behind them, they leave clean skins and teeth and white bones behind them, and these are tokens passed from one to another, so that the fugitive kind can always follow their kind.*

One of the actors had given Thelma and me a talking teddy bear each. These bears had a cord in the back and when you pulled it a series of phrases was delivered in a rather spooky, deep-throated American accent: 'I love you', 'My name's Teddy', and our favourite, 'Let's go to bed.' These sat on our desks and we pulled their cords regularly, much to Malcolm's annoyance: 'I'm going to confiscate those bears!' I believe Thelma still has hers; though his voice died long ago.

Thelma and I lived ten minutes away from one another and often travelled to work together. As I got into the car one morning she threw a powder compact at me. 'Darling, I've been trying to open this since last night, you'll have to take it back'; it was in fact tightly wrapped in clear plastic, which she had failed to notice.

For many years Thelma's glasses were heavy-rimmed – rather ahead of the curve, she preferred the kind of frames that have recently become very fashionable. These frames were in fact too heavy for her delicate features, and they would leave marks on the sides of her nose. In hot weather they would slide down her nose so she'd endlessly have to push them back into place. This was a major irritant for her, so one day she handed them to me and told me to find a way of making them stay in position. I got some fabric Elastoplast from the first-aid kit to fit round the bridge of the spectacles. She was delighted, they held in place. Malcolm said she looked crazy.

When I arrived one evening to collect her from her house for a first night we were attending, I found her all ready in her purple satin coat, tiara and matching shoes. 'I've had P. Hall on the phone for the last half hour – it's a wonder I'm ready at all, darling.' It wasn't until we were sitting in the stalls at the theatre that she nudged me in the ribs and asked me to remind her not to let anyone take her coat when we got to the party later. 'Why not?' I asked, at which point she showed me that she had nothing on but her bra and tights. She had put the coat on to come and answer the door when I arrived, and the dress she should have put on before Peter Hall rang was still hanging in the dry cleaner's bag on the back of her bathroom door.

# 9

## *It Worked in Cardboard*

'The child needs a Vitamin B12 injection, darling,' I heard Thelma say one morning, halfway through our first year of foreign visitors, before promptly marching me down to the basement where the resident nurse gave both of us the injection.

Peter Hall had promised Thelma she could present her very own World Theatre season as a kind of prize for making money with the tours and West End transfers. It was 1987. Though we would have all the facilities in the building at our disposal, Thelma would have to raise every penny necessary to bring six productions from four different countries for the first season, International 87. These visits began in April with Peter Stein's production of *The Hairy Ape*. Thelma had been inspired by Peter Daubeny's World Theatre Seasons at the Aldwych Theatre in the 1960s and 70s and was determined to do something that would match their breadth and scale. She succeeded, and received the Olivier/*Observer* Award for Outstanding Achievement in Theatre.

I cannot imagine that anyone who attended the press night of *The Hairy Ape* will ever forget the extraordinary spectacle of the coal-blackened men stripped to the waist, firing the liner which filled the Lyttelton Theatre. (Audience members in the first three rows were covered in coal dust during this scene – but nobody complained.)

Or the image of the industrialist's daughter, a ghostly white form descending the stairs to the boiler room. These scenes and other images provoked spontaneous applause during the very short run of this stunning production – there were only six performances. I didn't know this play by Eugene O'Neill and had not read it before I saw the production. Since it was performed in German, I understood nothing of what was said. But it's interesting; what happens when you take away language means the other senses are heightened, the story takes a visceral hold and you connect more than seems possible without words. Waves of understanding and feeling; it was like a dream in black and white.

'Nobody helps, nobody cares, you can never get hold of anybody,' said Peter Daubeny – a quote which was stuck up on our office wall and referred to on a daily basis during the mounting of these productions. After Thelma began her search for money she didn't stop asking for meetings and lunches with the heads of corporations from Mercedes-Benz to Glenfiddich whisky, until the target was reached. A deal with the Hilton Hotel chain was also negotiated and I was dispatched to look at various hotels and check rooms, and liaise with unsuspecting managers who had little idea they were about to have to cope with anything from Bergman's leading actor being too long for the hotel beds, to the Japanese leading actress demanding one hundred bags of ice cubes when a back injury called for a strange Japanese healing ritual. The most dramatic of these episodes would involve a member of one visiting company having a temper tantrum in a foyer after a major cocaine binge.

It was Thelma who taught me that when the budget allowed for £35 per night per person for hotel rooms, I should look pained and say our maximum was £25. We would then settle at £30 and I would beg for breakfast to be included. The first time I achieved this I was inordinately happy because Thelma was so impressed and it meant more money in the coffers for the first-night party.

With the help of the various cultural attachés at embassies – and, in the case of the Japanese, the Japan Foundation – we managed to secure interpreters for each production. We would require a minimum of four for each visit and they were most needed in the technical departments. We paid very little indeed, though they did receive vouchers for lunch and their travel expenses.

Most, however, did it for the experience. Our favourite Russian interpreter was Helen Molchanoff, who worked on the first season and with whom we would continue to work over the years. Helen had met Thelma when, as a student, she was interpreting at the Edinburgh Festival in 1979 for Robert Sturua's production of *Richard III*.

It didn't take long for a fever of excitement to grip the building. We made signs in the language of each visiting country so that they could all find their way from the stage door to the stage, from the dressing rooms to the canteen, to Wigs and Wardrobe. As soon as the signs went up, everyone from the post room to the Director's Office became aware that we were about to host an influx of eighty Germans, or one hundred and three Japanese. The canteen would lay on extra food, the bar would order extra beer and every department would prepare to work with their foreign counterparts.

Compared with the months of work preparing for a visit, the few days of performances were intense and all too short. The hype for the German production was particularly big as we were beset by technical problems that became national news, with Thelma appearing on a late-night BBC television bulletin. The fleet of forty-foot lorries containing the huge sets arrived five days before our first performance and it soon became apparent that the sets would not fit the stage. This catastrophe quickly bonded the English and German crews, who worked several overnights. Lucio Fanti, Peter Stein's designer, came to our office with Peter for a crisis meeting. What would happen if we couldn't make it work in time for the first performance? Fanti was over six feet tall, with thick shiny shoulder-length brown hair, always dressed in black and decidedly cool. He merely shrugged and said in a thick Italian accent, 'It worked in cardboard.' Ultimately the technicians had to weld two sections together so that it was possible for the side of the ship to open and reveal the inner workings of the boiler room.

On the day of the first performance, Thelma lay on the floor at the back of the Lyttelton Theatre, rosary beads in one hand, the other gesticulating wildly at the stage for the ship to open. The curtain was due to go up at 7 p.m. on the press night. It finally went up at 8.15. Thelma took the press to Ovations, the theatre restaurant and bar, and Malcolm and I were instructed to give everyone wine. We had more problems in the interval, which swelled from fifteen to forty-five minutes. But by the end, the audience was on their feet and the production was a triumph. The little black books made to look like artist's sketchbooks containing reproductions of Lucio Fanti's sketches for the set designs sold out during the interval on the first night, and with no more available, became collectable items.

After the performance, we had laid on a buffet with hot food and drink for the entire cast and crew, plus sponsors and those who had helped to make it all possible. Sometime after midnight, with the room spinning and the music booming out as exhausted technicians got more and more drunk, I swiped my security card and made my way backstage to collect our first-night gifts before heading home. It was two o'clock in the morning by the time we got to bed, but we would still need to be in our office early the next morning. We were busy with the final preparations for Ingmar Bergman's company, who would follow hard on the heels of the Germans with *Hamlet* and *Miss Julie*.

Sometimes during the foreign work it would be a struggle to be at the theatre every night. I'd want to, but I would also feel very tired, almost ill at times. One evening, probably coming down with something, I phoned Mum. I told her it was going to be a late night but that I felt very rough. She told me to go to the bar, order half a pint of Guinness and a glass of port. I was to drink half the Guinness, pour in the port and then drink that too. 'Just the one, it will pep you up.' It did, I forgot all about feeling poorly.

On nights like this I didn't always eat properly either. If I was going home mid-evening, I would stop off at Budgens on Bishop's Bridge Road, and if I was feeling really tired I would blow my budget and head for Marks & Spencer in the new Whiteleys on Queensway before heading home dizzy and weighed down with shopping bags. On the Tube one evening everything started to swim, I felt myself falling and clung to the pole, then fell sideways onto a man, apologised and wobbled off the Tube and up the platform, convinced that at any moment I was going to collapse. All manner of horrors gripped my mind. I clung to the side of the escalator and sweated. The following morning I made an appointment to see the doctor, who told me I'd had a panic attack. I had never heard of a panic attack and didn't consider myself to have been in a panic. 'I'd have a panic attack if I worked for the Honey Monster full time,' said Hodie (this was his nickname for Thelma).

Peter Stormare, Bergman's Hamlet, arrived at the stage door in tight black leather trousers, a T-shirt cut down to just below his chest, a studded black leather jacket, boots with heels that elevated him at least two inches above his six-foot-four-inch frame and fingernails painted black. All this was too exciting for Linda on stage door. She rang our office to say there was a very strange-looking man asking for Thelma. She couldn't pronounce his surname, but we finally worked out who it was and I was dispatched to collect him. It was love at first sight. He was a combination of kooky and handsome, his charisma was intoxicating and I developed a massive crush.

As Thelma would note, he was in fact the vision of the young Bergman, mercifully without Bergman's cantankerous nature. When Thelma had been to see the productions in Stockholm, Bergman had got up at one point and made his way towards a woman who was coughing. He stood in front of her glaring and said, 'Sick people should not come to the theatre.'

This production of *Hamlet* was one of the most cinematic pieces of theatre I have ever seen. When Fortinbras's army smashed through the back wall at the end wearing black motorcycle helmets with ghetto blasters on their shoulders, and rock music filled the auditorium while Hamlet died in Horatio's arms, I was never able to hold back my tears. Bergman's Ophelia came on in hobnailed boots and brandishing bent six-inch nails, not flowers. In the second Bergman production, *Miss Julie*, you could smell the bacon when Kristin cooks Jean his breakfast, rattling the pots and pans on the kitchen range. These productions were theatrical magic, and I felt that if I never saw another version of either *Hamlet* or *Miss Julie* it wouldn't matter because I had seen the definitive of each.

The productions were sold out, so Thelma and I would spend most of the evening in the 'Hostility Room', where we could watch the shows on a monitor. During our favourite bits we would sneak into the back of the auditorium. I cannot now listen to Samuel Barber's Adagio for Strings without being immediately transported back to the Lyttelton Theatre, to the moment when in Ninagawa's production Duncan kills Macbeth – in this instance, with one swipe of a samurai sword, where he appeared to be cut in half as the cherry blossom fell – and if I close my eyes I can still feel the seats, smell the auditorium and see parts of the performance with peculiar clarity. My stomach lurched and an adrenalised surge of emotion would take hold of me and I knew for certain that I would never see anything like this again. In the words of the critic Michael Billington, interviewed for a documentary about Ninagawa's work, 'It shed a whole new light on *Macbeth*, not as some crime and punishment melodrama, but as a play about the sadness of all earthly things.'

Entertaining in the Hostility Room could be a fraught experience as people stood around nervously waiting to be offered drinks, unsure of what to say to whom, and silence could be misread for a lack of appreciation. Except, in that first season, there was only a constant flow of praise. Edna O'Brien sweeping in, full of bonhomie, and telling me how much she liked my shoes was a highlight, mainly because the shoes were the only things I was wearing that weren't hand-me-downs from Thelma. I had wanted to meet Edna ever since I had been party to the immortal line she delivered to a mutual friend – 'There's not an hour goes by I don't think of Chekhov.' This became one of our stock phrases.

By the time we had hosted all but the final visit, it was clear that the season had been a huge success. We closed with the Mayakovsky company in a Russian play called *Tomorrow Was War* by Boris Vasiliev.

Thelma hated surtitles and had refused to have them for any of the previous productions in this season. She believed a good programme note and a proper synopsis would suffice, and frankly she was horrified at the notion that people did not know the story of *Macbeth* or *Medea*. She had to make an exception in the case of this last play, as nobody knew anything about it. She agreed to a simultaneous translation, which would be transmitted live to the audience during each production and read by her friend Vanessa Redgrave. At one performance, just as 'the half' (the half hour before the curtain goes up) had been called, Vanessa ran into the Green Room where she had been told she could find the stage manager, who was having a drink before the show. Vanessa was in a total panic as upon arrival at the theatre she discovered that she'd left her script at home.

With only half an hour before the curtain was due to go up, this was something of a disaster. The stage manager calmed her down, persuading her there was no time for her to return home. Instead she would take Vanessa's car keys and address in order to go and retrieve the script. For the first half hour of the performance Vanessa gave a simultaneous translation entirely from memory. On her return, the stage manager then tiptoed into the director's box, slipped the script into Vanessa's hands, who then calmly found her place and continued.

The director, Alexander Goncharov, was billed thus in the programme: *A. A. Goncharov People's Artist of the USSR, Winner of the State Prize of the USSR and the RSFSR*. His wife would barge into the Lyttelton Theatre during rehearsals and start shouting at him. We discovered from Helen, our interpreter, that she was insisting he accompany her shopping in Oxford Street. '*Machina, machina!*' she would bark, meaning that she expected a car to be at her disposal.

There were lots of men in grim suits who'd come and stand in our office smoking very strong, unpleasant-smelling cigarettes. Malcolm put his foot down very quickly about this as he couldn't bear either the smoke or the constant shouting and demands while we tried to work. 'That's it!' he would say. 'Get out, get out, get out, all of you – out!' The bemused men would hover in the corridor and Thelma would send me down to the stage to find Helen in order to understand what they were talking about. They usually wanted something. '*Machina*,' they would repeat almost daily, and we would explain that they had to use the bus and the Underground and that was what their per diems were for. The young actors never complained; it was always the gaggle of men who Thelma referred to as the KGB. We were never entirely sure what their roles were, and there were certainly too many of them. We did also feel sorry for them, in their bad suits and their constant desire to go shopping in Oxford Street. C&A and Marks & Spencer were for them the Holy Grails of consumerism.

We fell in love with each company and thought we would never feel the same again, until the next one arrived. I was only just acclimatising myself to the fickle nature of life in the theatre. I remember Thelma firing a glance at Malcolm, – as if to say 'Don't say anything else' – when he asked why I was crying when we all met in the Hostility Room on the final night. I knew she had felt the same, and I knew that she still felt a version of it, albeit without my undisciplined reservoir of emotion.

The day the Russians left, Thelma, Helen and I accompanied them on the coach to the airport. I cried again, and Thelma took us for a curry en route back to London. It was a terrible curry full of peas in some bleak place by a roundabout. She treated the coach driver as well. I think she felt he had become emotionally involved in our brief encounter.

Thelma had only two tickets to the Olivier Awards and so she took Malcolm. She felt badly that she couldn't take me too because I had worked so hard, but we all had and Malcolm had been with her far longer than my two years. I didn't mind, I watched it on television and as soon as I heard Donald Trelford (then Editor of the *Observer*) say 'For breaking down barriers, for releasing us from our insularity . . . ' I knew that it was Thelma and not Barry Humphries who had won the award. The next thing I heard was her thanking Malcolm and me. It was the only time she ever used my original name. Just before getting up to receive the award she had nudged Malcolm in the ribs and said, 'What's Sweetpea's real name!?'

I ran all the way down Westbourne Grove with a string of balloons and a big sign I had made and pinned them all to her door to await her late return.

# 10

## *Two Left Boots*

The number 23 bus went from Paddington to the Aldwych; I'd jump off (in those days you could jump off a moving bus) at the traffic lights at the top of the Strand and walk over Waterloo Bridge. I preferred this journey to the Tube, but it did take considerably longer.

On this particular morning the wind was incredibly strong and by the time I reached the start of the bridge I was walking with some effort against a gale. By the time I got to the middle of the bridge my long black winter coat was billowing out behind me and threatened to carry me up and off my feet. I was suddenly nervous and moved to the edge of the bridge and, holding on tight to the railings, looked down to the choppy brown waters of the Thames below. It was then that I spotted the two businessmen up ahead, down on the ground clinging to the railings with one hand, briefcases in the other. They were shouting at me to 'get down' – which I did immediately. The wind was stronger than ever and standing up was out of the question. The three of us began a slow, crawling progress along the remainder of the bridge, all the while clutching the rails.

I arrived at our office at the National to find Penny at her desk, immaculate as ever. She was on the phone and smiled and waved at me as I entered. It seemed ridiculous to try and recount what had just happened. Anyway, Thelma was far too exercised by the arrival of a long cardboard box and a letter in Russian. She was waving the letter as she summoned me with her customary 'Come here, Pealet – I've got a job for you.'

Six weeks had passed since we'd waved the Mayakovsky company goodbye. The long cardboard box contained two left boots – long black suede boots with a heel and fur trim at the top – and a request that we take these boots back to C&A on Oxford Street and exchange one of the left boots for a right boot.

Thelma gave me her business card, the letter in Russian and the box of boots and told me not to come back without the right boot. She meant it too – when Jeanette Winterson was on work experience with her at the Roundhouse, Thelma sent her off to find two obscure lines of poetry and said the same to her. Jeanette was gone for two days. As I left she shouted, 'Don't speak to shop assistants, darling, go straight to the top, ask for the manager and tell them who we are.'

What I didn't know was at that time there were three C&A stores on Oxford Street. We had no receipt, and many weeks had passed since the purchase. I entered the first and asked for the manager. A female shop assistant said the manager was busy and asked what my problem was. I explained that I was from the National Theatre and that I had two left boots and a letter in Russian from the gentleman who had purchased them as a gift for his wife. This was clearly a first for her. She disappeared and was gone some time before returning to inform me that they had no odd boots in the store, that there was no way of telling if the boots had originally been purchased in that particular store and that I should proceed to the next C&A further up Oxford Street.

I arrived and introduced myself as the girl from the

National Theatre with the two left boots. I was sent to the second floor to queue at the information and returns desk, where they would be able to find out if an odd boot remained. There were two people in front of me. I was not aware of the first person's problem, but the one just in front of me was a woman returning with a brand-new bag she had purchased the previous day and which she was unable to open. It was rather like a doctor's bag, with many clasps, pockets, latches and buttons. The woman on the desk couldn't open it either, so she disappeared and returned with a male colleague who was also unsuccessful.

After much struggling, the three of them managed to get into the handbag. While this scene was playing out I was aware of a woman behind me who was agitated and kept moving beside me and then behind me, looking at her watch and muttering under her breath. I noticed that she was perspiring slightly and, eventually, having perhaps seen a sympathetic face, she told me she was parked outside and was concerned about her car. I offered her my place in the queue, I was not in a hurry. My concern was that I would not be welcomed back without the right boot. Actually, neither was I in a particular hurry to follow the handbag debacle with two left boots and a letter in Russian. I would be grateful for what looked like a straightforward returns job to normalise things.

The woman had a couple of suits over her arm, one brown and one blue. She was incredibly grateful and moved forward as the lady with the formerly sealed handbag left. She explained that her husband had bought the suits, but that they did not fit him. The woman on the desk looked at the suits, then at the woman, and then more closely at the suits. She then disappeared out the back.

I noticed that my fellow returnee was looking a little more agitated and was still perspiring.

The sales assistant returned with the suits. 'When did your husband buy these suits, madam?'

She was not sure.

'Well perhaps you could check and see if he has a receipt; it's just that they look rather old and it would appear that they have actually been altered.'

Silence.

'Would you like to check with your husband, madam?'

The reply came: 'He's dead, so I can't. I just thought maybe I could exchange them.'

The sales assistant looked stunned. She disappeared and returned with a manager who explained that they had not made these particular suits since the seventies and that unfortunately it would not be possible to exchange them.

By the time I opened my mouth to explain I had no receipt, two left boots and a letter in Russian, the poor sales assistant was reeling. Rather extraordinarily, they did have a lone right boot and I returned to my desk at the National with my head held high, having done, I thought, rather better than Jeanette Winterson.

I was full of myself and headed to Dorset for the weekend. My brother was already there and picked me up from a station very close to our maternal grandparents'. My grandmother had advanced Alzheimer's at this stage. When we got there, Mum came straight out to meet us, looking very serious. 'There's nothing to be done, but I'm just warning you: she thinks you are Lady Diana coming for tea, so all the best china is out.' When I went in she got up and curtsied. As we all sat sipping tea, my grandmother couldn't take her eyes off me.

# 11

## *Dreams of Owning*

During the early years at Westbourne Terrace, Hodie and I would drive to Dorset for weekends every now and then in his very first car, which was an old Ford Cortina estate. Leaving London as early as we could on a Friday evening, it was always a thrill to see the sun setting behind Stonehenge. Having worked well and hard all week we had plenty of news and tales of the city for our parents. It was beautiful there; I loved walking and going down to the sea, but was far too excited by London and by my work to imagine the possibility of ever living there again.

When we returned to London on a Sunday evening, nothing was ever open, except the Nisa store in Praed Street. I'd buy a bottle of water and a pint of milk in a Tetra carton and butterflies would gather in my stomach at the prospect of a new week.

One Sunday, just as we drew up in Praed Street, the car stopped and wouldn't restart. Hodie had to be at Pinewood early the following morning; he had just started working for a construction manager helping to build and decorate sets. He needed the car, which was loaded with things from Dorset. Produce from my mother, eggs, vegetables, cider which they bought from a local farm, a couple of old rugs, a chair and two bronze sculptures rescued from my father's studio – he had intended to melt them down. Hodie was close to tears of utter frustration when it seemed certain the car wouldn't start. Somehow we managed to push it up the hill and on to Eastbourne Terrace and then down the incline that is Chilworth Street. Miraculously, with me pushing and him at the wheel, the car finally started and we got to Westbourne Terrace and unloaded our treasure.

The flat always felt reinvigorated when we brought things back from Dorset, items Mum and Dad were getting rid of, or things we picked up cheaply in the market. Now everything is called 'vintage' and far more expensive than it ever was then. As Hodie's earnings increased, the cars got better and soon we would be making the journey in a DIY reconditioned, re-sprayed Saab. As time passed, it became harder to return to London on Sundays, with the butterflies in my stomach turning to knots.

Arriving home after work one evening, I found the flat in darkness and the door ajar, which was odd as we always double-locked – but the lock didn't appear to have been forced. I pushed it gingerly and called out. No reply. Entering the sitting room, I realised something was wrong. The television and video recorder were unplugged and had been left marooned in the middle of the floor. I then discovered my bedroom had been ransacked and three beautiful leather jackets given to me by my mother from her collection were gone. These were the most valuable grown-up clothes I possessed.

Upstairs, I cautiously entered Hodie's room to find him sound asleep. After some prodding and shouting he eventually came to. He had been suffering from a severe cold and the previous night had taken a good dose of Night Nurse, consequently sleeping through the entire incident.

We were frightened by the break-in so all of us in the flat that night slept in the same room, with the hall light on. Our burglar turned out to be the spurned lover of a previous flatmate, this being his revenge for my asking him to move out. Later he was put on a restraining order by the police, which was just as well as two of Thelma's technicians at the National had offered to 'take care' of the situation for me.

We were by now in need of two new flatmates and by some good fortune I managed to find them both within a matter of days.

I was having tea with Harry downstairs when in walked a Marlon Brando lookalike called Charlie. I was so stunned by his looks that I sat with my mouth open, speechless, while he and Harry chatted about paintings by Charlie's brother Oliver. Oliver, whom I'd already met, was renting a room from Harry, and Charlie had come to deliver some canvases for him. 'Who was that?' I said, trying not to seem overly interested as he disappeared along the terrace. Harry thought he might be looking for somewhere to rent as he had just got a place at Saint Martins. He was getting bored, commuting from his parents' home in Tunbridge Wells. She gave me his number and I called him the next day from the National.

My enthusiasm for Charlie's good looks had nothing to do with sexual attraction, although at the time I was trying very hard to find boys sexually attractive, and even had a boyfriend. Oliver had introduced us at a party and I found him instantly fascinating. Tom was very different from the boys I was used to, who all wore dirty 501s, T-shirts, Doc Martens, and smoked marijuana. He wore suits made at Gieves & Hawkes and Church's brogues with little metal things stuck on the soles, so he could always be heard approaching with a very grown-up clip-a-dee-clop. He smoked strong cigarettes, drank spirits and wore a vintage Biba watch.

Although the same age as the rest of us, Tom appeared older, not just because of the clothes, the deep and booming posh voice, but on account of his general air of sophistication. Resembling a slightly less good-looking version of Rupert Everett, he had an ample slick of hair which was regularly tossed to one side.

It was Tom who introduced me to the next new flatmate. Fifi, with her mass of golden curls, reminded me of Carole King. Half Norwegian and half English, Fifi was full of nervous energy and possessed a manic infectious laugh. Just back from a year's trip around the world – which for someone who had only been to France and once to Majorca, was very impressive – she had nowhere to live. Arriving with one batik fabric holdall and a bedroll, she had a habit of sleeping on the floor, which had much to do with her time in India. Fifi was a great cook and was now earning her living working for an exclusive agency, preparing dishes for private and corporate dinner parties. That we shared a love of reading was a bonus, added to which she and Tom were very close.

Tom and I were intellectually compatible and blessed with a similar sense of humour, but I had no sexual desire whatsoever. One evening I agreed to look at his penis in the vain hope that this might elicit some hitherto unlocked desire. Unfortunately, when he flumped it out, it had absolutely the reverse effect. I liked the idea of boys, particularly boys who looked like Tom and Charlie, but wasn't liberated enough to accept my sexuality and consequently wasted a lot of time. I had a very good relationship with an artist at the time, though our friendship was put to the test when he declared his love for me over a plate of pasta in Soho. I told him it was impossible for me to reciprocate, that I had a boyfriend, but he insisted and so as a desperate measure I surprised myself by telling him that women were more attractive to me. He dismissed this by ignoring it and banged the table with his fist saying, 'You are in denial!' I was in denial, but not about him.

I was a late developer. My glamorous Grandma Peggy, bothered by this, sent me a bust-developer one Christmas. A strange inflatable object which had to be squeezed at each end in order to turn one into Brigitte Bardot. I hadn't worried about this late development, at least not until she sent the bust developer. In the sixth form a boy had told me that sex was a 'dirty, smelly and painful process'. Sometime later I noticed a girlfriend limping to school, and was perplexed and appalled to discover this was as a result of a sexual tryst with the boy in question. I decided that for the time being my head was the best place for such intimacies to occur. Indeed, for some time I lived, as Sir Richard Francis Burton once said of the average educated Victorian woman, 'in a rustle of imaginary copulation'.

At school I enjoyed hanging out with boys, and I had some very good boy 'friends' who were also keen on music, books and films. However, social evenings that strayed into uncharted territory, usually involving alcohol, ended badly for me. On one such evening I'd been invited to a party by one of my sixth-form friends. Later that evening I found myself crawling around his parents' garden, vomiting, unable to stand and uncertain of where I was. The garden appeared to be on a steep incline, but a later visit revealed a perfectly flat expanse of lawn neatly delineated with rose bushes. Mr Smith drove me home and on opening the passenger door I fell out on to a pile of sandstone, recently delivered for one of Dad's building projects, and was immediately sick. Hodie tried to get me up and into the house, and during this manoeuvre I became separated from my shoes, which Mr Smith drove over as he left. Unable to get me upstairs, Hodie put me on the sofa, then rolled the kelim rugs up and thoughtfully placed a bucket strategically to hand.

When Mum came down the following morning and found me covered in blood, vomit and bruises, she was convinced I had been assaulted.

This modus operandi extended for the next few years, and was followed by a rather complicated phase as I renewed my efforts to find boys attractive. In some instances this was successful, but only in a superficial sense. A combination of alcohol and a desire to be 'normal' led to an embarrassing number of close encounters in my bedroom. Most of these trysts involved my pretending to have passed out and trying not to move while untrained hands roamed over my virgin frame. Tom didn't push me physically, and because I genuinely enjoyed his company we became involved in a mutually beneficial but confining alliance. I do believe he was tormented by our relationship and had I been more evolved at the time I would never have let it continue so unresolved.

Charlie moved in the following week. When his father delivered him and his belongings, he took me aside and warned me of Charlie's gift for domestic chaos. I chose not to focus on this as Charlie was so beautiful, and as it turned out a fabulous cook. I had given him the flat rules: clean up, no parties, pay rent on time.

The weekend after he moved in I was in Dorset, so I asked Hodie and Fifi to show him the pantry in the kitchen and explain how it worked. The pantry was a large floor-to-ceiling cupboard that filled an entire wall with five long, wide shelves. We had a shelf each for our own food and a communal shelf for things like washing-up liquid, loo rolls and other household items considered necessary – for these we operated a kitty. Hodie called me, sounding as if something terrible had happened. Charlie had apparently taken it upon himself to rearrange all the shelves, putting all our produce together. 'Why didn't you tell him about the pantry!' I shouted.

Despite this, Hodie and Charlie were soon inseparable and regularly had parties for two at the flat. Parties for two quickly became parties for three when Oliver, now ensconced downstairs in Harry's flat, occupied one of our empty rooms as a painting studio. From now on the innocent days of pot-smoking were replaced with an apparently more sophisticated drug of choice. For my brother, a young man working on film sets and doing regular all-nighters, the piles of cocaine seemed as commonplace as tea and coffee in a rehearsal room, and the temptation was all too intense. Visiting him while he was house-sitting for an art director he worked with, I marvelled at the stylish accommodation and was particularly struck by the waist-high pillars made of steel with mirrors on top. There were four of these and I walked around looking down at myself. 'Why does he have all these mirrors like this?' I said. Hodie collapsed laughing.

Hodie worked long hours and sometimes, like me, weekends were included. The work ethic had been instilled in us from an early age and by the time I was sixteen we both had jobs in the local pub-restaurant just a few miles from our home in Dorset. My first tasks were washing up and peeling hundreds of carrots for hours on end in a freezing outdoor garage. I was soon promoted to waitress, which I hated more than the washing up and peeling carrots. I'd hoped that falling on the bread trolley and ending up in hospital with cracked ribs and having to be cut out of my uniform would result in my demotion. It didn't, and even when I upset the three-tiered dessert trolley on a piece of loose carpet, watching in horror as every pudding I had just named to the expectant customers slid off and crashed to the ground in slow motion, I remained gainfully employed.

Hodie was the most organised, clean and tidy of all the young men I lived with. In the days before we could afford a washing machine he would often accompany me to the launderette – a short walk down Bishop's Bridge Road – where for £3.50 we got a service wash. One lovely spring day as we walked along, chatting as we carried our loaded bags, I felt a flapping and scratching inside my baggy sweatpants.

I dropped my bag and screamed, 'Hodie, Hodie, get it out, get it out!'

He stood staring at me, shouting, 'What's happening?! Get what out?'

'The bird!' I shrieked. 'There's a bird in my trousers!'

Dropping to his knees, he stretched the elasticated ankle wide, at which point the laundry ticket fell out of my trousers, having worked its way down from a hole in the pocket. 'Jesus, Pea, you really need to get a grip on this bird thing.'

I went back later that afternoon to collect the laundry, but mine had been stolen – virtually all my clothes gone in an instant. Richard Eyre, eventually Peter Hall's successor as Director of the National Theatre, gave me a pair of his 501s and Thelma had another wardrobe clear-out: 'We need a whip-round, darlings – the child has no clothes!'

I worked hard to make the flat nice, single-handedly ripping up carpets and varnishing wooden floors. I'm impatient, and as the place wasn't ours I was loath to spend money I didn't have doing more than was necessary to give the illusion of sophistication. Removing the carpets made a huge difference, though, and I stripped down some doors with a burner, which produced an interesting effect.

A decorator friend said it wasn't worth painting the main living rooms as there were so many cracks and gaps it would show everything up and make it look worse. So I put up some large paintings Oliver had in his studio and which he lent me, plus any old production photographs I got from work, thus breaking up the huge wall space and at the same time covering offending areas. Most of the offending areas were patches of wall where I had previously attempted to hang a work. Having failed to get a nail in at the desired position, I would try several inches to the left, right, up or down until I found a receptive patch of wall. The resultant mass of holes and missing chunks of plaster enraged Hodie. 'That's an external wall!' he would yell. 'It needs a drill and a masonry bit – you lash-up Annie!'

With the help of a friendly production manager, I procured a faux Georgian sofa in cream and gold. Boys and serially unwashed jeans don't go with cream, but I loved it. In addition, I had two old chairs from a production, a bit rickety but good-looking. At weekends we would wander up and down the Portobello Road looking at all the bric-a-brac and antiques, most of which was out of our league. Occasionally I would find something affordable, like the two candelabras each holding five candles and large enough not to look out of place on the enormous table we had inherited with the flat. These I would light most evenings, even if I was alone; it was synonymous with relaxing and for me a night when nobody was in was a gift. I would sit at the little table in front of my bedroom window, looking out over the back of Gloucester Terrace, typing what I am quite sure was rather indifferent poetry. There was a woman opposite who had a very well appointed studio flat. She was usually alone and I envied her peace and the order of things, which I could clearly see through the glass doors onto her immaculate roof terrace decorated with pots of lavender.

This occasional peace was short-lived; any number of keys in the lock would herald the return of boys with bottles, and then chaos would ensue. There was no possibility, on my salary, of a well-appointed studio flat. But it got me thinking: what if Hodie and I bought

somewhere between us? We looked into this for pre-
cisely one day. We drove to an estate agent and told
him what we thought we could afford between us. He
produced a piece of paper with a grim-looking flat in
a block somewhere called Norwood. Hodie walked out
immediately, leaving me to say we would think about
it. Outside he said, 'Norwood! I'd rather live in fucking
Norway.'

That evening we sat in post-property-ownership-
illusion gloom, watching a bad film about a porn star
with a ridiculous name. As we got drunker, Hodie began
coming up with his own Hollywood-inspired porn star
names and in rapid succession gleefully announced:
'Anchovy Quim! . . . Smegory Pecker! . . . Spurt Wancas-
ter!' I couldn't think of any.

# 12

## Tales Out of Touring

As his swansong at the National, Peter Hall announced that he would direct three late Shakespeare plays: *Cymbeline*, *The Tempest* and *A Winter's Tale*. These would also tour to Russia and Japan. A single company of actors would perform all three. The cast included Sarah Miles, Eileen Atkins and Tim Pigott-Smith. Thelma predicted 'a very rocky ride indeed'.

Sarah Miles was the replacement for a young actress who had just given birth. Over a weekend Peter met Sarah at a dinner party with the writer Robert Bolt, her husband. Peter was impressed, even though she was significantly older than the original casting and had a reputation for being eccentric – as I was about to find out.

In the build-up to a tour it was quite usual for me to have to pursue actors endlessly around the building to fill in visa forms and get passports renewed. Most tricky of all was getting them to a photo booth for their passport shot for visa forms. Sarah Miles was almost impossible to catch. I finally cornered her in the NT canteen. She was bizarrely attired in what appeared to be a large Babygro in vibrant red, with a huge Russian fur hat, several handbags, and a small dog under her arm. Dogs were definitely not allowed in the building, and most certainly not the canteen. In addition, someone had stuck a great big notice on the door saying 'NO

DOGS ALLOWED IN THE CANTEEN OR GREEN ROOM'. Everyone in the building knew that this sign was directed at one person only. I have no idea why someone didn't speak on the matter directly to Sarah; perhaps they did and it fell on deaf ears, as did my pleas to her for signatures on forms and photographs. But here she was, and I approached her with a form and a pen at the ready. Refusing to use my pen, she struggled with the dog and the jumble of bags to find her Mont Blanc, before turning to me and saying loudly, 'Oh, I've just burped pickled onions in your face!'

One evening in our office after rehearsals and through a cloud of cigar smoke, Peter Hall expressed concern to Thelma about the casting of Sarah Miles. Though worried, she reiterated the consensus that Sarah was a film actress for whom the transition to stage clearly required careful handling, and given more concentrated time under Peter's guidance, it was hoped she would turn a corner. This was not to be. At a run-through of the play in Rehearsal Room 1 the following Saturday, the whole thing seemed to be falling apart. Peter phoned Thelma from the canteen and after solemn discussion asked her to replace Sarah.

Geraldine James was cast on the Monday morning and had the Herculean task of learning and rehearsing Imogen in *Cymbeline* in just two weeks. I put Sarah's incomplete visa application in the bin. Then I began making the phone calls necessary to enlist help from the highest levels at the various embassies in order to expedite Geraldine's visas, given the short notice.

In those days, without email or scanning machines, Rosie and I had actually to visit embassies and would sit at tables with passports piled high while each individual form was surveyed and receipts issued for our applications. There were well over a hundred of these, including all actors, crew and creative team. We would have to wait days, and despite Thelma's considerable contacts at the various embassies they were often only issued at the eleventh hour. I would have sleepless nights worrying about half-finished forms, missing photographs, and, most of all, lost passports. These I would lock up each evening in a large drawer in my desk. I only ever mislaid one passport and one set of photographs; unfortunately, they belonged to the same actor. It made me break out into a sweat even to contemplate having to tell him, and the weight of work I considered to be nothing short of CIA operative-status sat heavy on my shoulders.

The pressure on Peter Hall, the actors and the entire team to have the productions open to the public according to schedule was immense. One evening in the Cottesloe, during a lengthy technical dress rehearsal, Peter lost his temper. This was a very rare event and therefore all the more shocking. It concerned a severed head on top of a pole, which unintentionally resembled Ken Dodd. I suspect that this was more a case of what Thelma describes as 'moving furniture about on the *Titanic*'; the real problems were elsewhere. The design for the three plays relied on a revolving split set, one half of which would fold upwards to create a wall, the other half remaining as floor. This installation was operated by hydraulics, which would invariably break down. The result was that scene changes, which should have taken seconds, sometimes lasted minutes, and even hours.

Meanwhile, Geraldine James, pale with anxiety, sat

with Thelma and me at the back of the theatre. I knew of Geraldine, having seen her in the television series, *The Jewel in the Crown*. I came to believe that she could play absolutely any character and she was always on any casting list drawn up in our office over the years, though sadly she was rarely available.

Thelma was at her best during a crisis, with a frenzy of energy, including the ability to stay up all night if necessary and still keep her sense of humour. She and Peter Hall seemed to be a dream team, and despite the endless deficit at the National in those days, there was certainly no poverty of imagination. Thelma pressed a wad of cash into my hand and dispatched me to the Green Room with an order to buy drinks for everyone. Soon the atmosphere became less tense and I watched as Thelma climbed over the seats to reach Peter, put her arms around his neck and whispered something reassuring in his ear.

The rehearsals in the Cottesloe continued to be a nightmare, and what was meant to be the first preview of *The Tempest* became a public 'technical dress rehearsal' to a fully booked auditorium. Peter gave instructions that, should there be any complaints, the box office would issue full refunds. Nobody asked for their money back.

Thelma's ability to ride a crisis was matched by her affection for actors and directors. It extended to every aspect of their life in the theatre and on the road. Before each tour I would produce travel schedules detailing exactly where everyone had to be and when, and she would write a four- or five-page letter to the entire company giving them as much detail as she could about each destination. She would always have been on a recce to the venues with the production manager in advance of any tour, forensically checking all accommodation and facilities at the theatres. When I look back on some of these documents, I marvel at the way we cosseted everyone. Thelma believed in repeating information as many times as possible to actors, a strategy based on her observation, 'They're all children, darling.' There certainly seemed to be a collective abandonment of responsibility on the part of many actors. I would regularly take calls from those departing asking me how to find Terminal 2, or the Air France check-in. I did wonder how they ever managed to go on holiday. Here are some extracts from the letter she wrote to the Late Shakespeares company in May 1988:

*Dear All*
*At the risk of repeating myself, I am going to put on paper some of the things I think you ought to know about our forthcoming tour.*

*Because of the ungodly hour we are departing from London on Thursday, 26 May – this is because of the time difference in Moscow where they are three hours ahead of us – we are not assembling at the South Bank. You will each make your own way by private transport to Heathrow Airport, Terminal 2, Air France check-in desk. We are checking in as a group, which means we have someone there to speed us through. He will be waiting for you with Sweetpea and Rosie, and he will give all your tickets to Rosie who will hand out boarding passes when they are processed. The Air France ticket desk is the farthest on the right when you come into the building, i.e. if you are outside and facing Terminal 2, you turn sharp right and the desk is at the very end. We must all check in by 6.30 a.m. in order to catch the flight No. AF807. It is, therefore, essential that you are assembled for check-in not later than 6.20 a.m. On arrival at the Group Check-In, please give Sweetpea a receipt for your taxi (or whatever brought you to the airport) and she will refund you on the spot in sterling (which I daresay you will then spend in Duty Free!).*

She went on to give them details of their baggage allowance, and her predicted weather forecast for both Moscow and Tokyo, which she invented for the occasion. Following up with:

*I also recommend that you bring the following: your own soap, vitamin C, headache pills if you need them (Russian ones are lousy). Tampax if you use them – they are not available in the Soviet Union; eye masks (£1.20 from Boots) as all curtains in Russia are unlined and let in the early morning light, and although I hope that we will none of us be situated in noisy parts of our hotels, if you are sensitive to noise, take ear plugs. For those of you that shave, take enough for the entire time in the Soviet Union as their stuff smells funny. Contrary to rumour it is not necessary to take lavatory paper to the USSR. I always take an alarm clock because they forget to wake you up, and if you do not like using very thin, small towels, take one of those with you, although I never do.*

\*

And then:

> *Sleep with your colleagues if you must, but I strongly advise against chance encounters.*

Though fond of her charges, she was also firm. Hotels, she maintained, seemed to bring the worst out in people, characterised by a litany of moans and groans about perfectly decent accommodation. Thelma always said that while those who were used to a certain level of hotel didn't complain, others who could never have afforded such accommodation somehow felt they were entitled to nothing less than the Cipriani. Again, her strong feelings about how we should behave when spending taxpayers' money informed her decisions in this regard. Though never putting actors or technicians in poor hotels, and certainly nowhere she wouldn't stay herself, Thelma remained cost-conscious. However, this was not at the expense of the wellbeing of all company members:

> *The good news is that the per diems have been increased in Russia to 10 rubles and are not 8 as in your touring contract. The theatre we are playing is the MKHAT, No. 3. Proyesd Khudozhestvennovo, Moscow. The hotel we are staying in, God willing, is the Peking Hotel, Blvd. Sadovaya Ulitsa, 10–5, 103001 Moscow (tel: Moscow 209 0935), and this is situated 15/20 minutes' walking distance from the theatre. The Peking is a soft currency hotel. You will not be able to spend sterling or dollars there, but you do not have to pay for anything there other than your alcohol for the evening meal*

*(your breakfast and dinner are pre-arranged). If*
*you do not avail yourself of the catering facilities*
*laid on, then God knows what you will do, but you*
*cannot have the money instead, as we have to pay*
*up front for our food. (If the food is unspeakably*
*vile in Moscow, we will fight to make yet other*
*arrangements, and we shall only pay for the first*
*three days to see how we get on.)*

Without email or fax, and with the hit or miss of getting someone on the end of the phone who might speak
some English, preparations for the tour were protracted
and frustrating. I was giddy with a combination of excitement at the challenge and a chilling fear of making
even the smallest error. As the youngest and least
experienced member of the team, my eagerness ensured
that every coach booking, every plane ticket, every visa
form, would be checked countless times.

I waited outside the Russian Embassy in Kensington
Gate before it opened in the morning, to be first in to
deliver applications. Trying to ingratiate myself with
embassy staff turned out to be a pointless exercise. I
would press the buzzer. Nothing. I would press again.
This time a gruff voice would answer in Russian, to
which I would announce Telma Holt, dropping the 'h'
in Thelma at her instruction: 'Darling, you say "Telma",
not Thelma; the Russians understand Telma.' This was
consistent with what we referred to as 'Thelmaese' – her
own phonetic kind of language employed when dealing
with the Russians and the Japanese, often with hilari-
ous consequences.

I would then give the name of the Ambassador or
whomever Thelma had managed to ensnare. 'You wait,'

the voice would say. This meant standing there for another ten minutes before the buzzer would go to release
the gate. There was a conspiratorial atmosphere inside
the embassy. The men, dressed in brown nylon suits,
reeked of strong cigarettes, never smiled and everything
was done very, very slowly. I had the distinct impression
that there was a sly sense of satisfaction in making us
wait.

John Mortimer was one of three writers to accompany the National Theatre on the first part of the tour
to Moscow and Tbilisi. He was there to do an article
for the *Telegraph Weekend*. 'The child will look after
you,' Thelma said as she marched him towards my desk,
instructing me to sort out all his travel and 'Make sure
he has a quiet room at the hotel, darling.' I knew who
John Mortimer was immediately; in fact, he was so rec-
ognisable to me that his presence in our office seemed
somehow incongruous – he was almost a character, not
a real person. I had read his book *Paradise Postponed*
and watched the television adaptation with two more of
my favourite actors, Zoë Wanamaker and David Threl-
fall. His charm and his wit made this particular task a
pleasure. 'Won't you come with me?' he pleaded. 'How
will I manage out there without you? I shall need you to
look after me.'

Sadly, the truth was that I never got further than
Heathrow or Gatwick Airport. There simply wasn't the
budget for it. By the time they left the country, my work
was done and from that point they had Thelma, Rosie
and a team of stage management to look after them.

Waving them off at the airport was always an anti-
climax. I'd make my way forlornly back to the National

on the Tube and sit at my desk, eagerly awaiting news. I missed Thelma hugely because all the mad life she brought into the office was replaced by the ordinary daily grind that was Malcolm and me just getting on with whatever was required. It was very quiet and rather dull when she wasn't there generating action and adventure.

London was dirtier and darker in the eighties. Always littered, chewing-gum stamped into the pavements, road sweepers with their trolleys and wide brushes sweeping up the endless detritus. One evening during the early part of Thelma's absence, I left the National and walked down what was then an underpass to Waterloo Station. This journey was marked by the smell of urine and the same homeless characters who, rather like buskers, had their preferred spots. One in particular stood out for me: a woman in her sixties who stood staring straight ahead, speaking and singing. Once well dressed and still well spoken, a grey bob with a hair slide always in the same place, she spoke pure Beckett and I wondered what fault lines had given way to bring her here. Was life really that precarious? Could I ever end up like that? I bought a copy of the *Evening Stand-ard* and sat down on the Tube, which seemed always to smell of stale cigarettes, the discarded butts filling the gaps between the wooden slats in the floor. There was a short report of a young actress who had killed herself; I recognised the name, I'd heard the girls in Casting talking about her.

At the National the clock ticked slowly. I longed for calls from Moscow, but as ever calls to London were tricky for the group and, apart from Thelma, only Rosie had a phone in her room that worked for international calls. So people rang her to pass on messages to the actors. As a result, she had many conversations with Eileen Atkins's husband. This prompted Eileen to tease Rosie with the question, 'Are you having an affair with my husband?!'

There was no one better behaved than Rosie, but in those days it seemed that affairs on tour were a common occurrence. Much like excessive drinking, it was as though everyone felt they were suddenly permitted to abandon all self-restraint, as if what happened on tour was somehow not real life. The very fact of being part of a temporary exile from the homeland was licence to throw caution to the wind.

Rosie's dispatches rarely disappointed. My favourite was the time she and Thelma were woken at 2 a.m. by hotel staff informing them that an actor was running naked around the hotel, banging on people's doors.

When Thelma managed to get a call through to us from Moscow, she would half-whisper everything, convinced her room had been 'bugged', and became almost inaudible when she had something very important to say. 'I can't hear you, Thelma,' I pleaded, desperately concerned that I was missing crucial instructions. 'I can't shout, Pea, the KGB are probably listening.'

The first week of the tour in Moscow was fairly uneventful; the only drama seemed to be that breakfast and dinner were always exactly the same meal: hard-boiled eggs, caviar and cold meat. Rosie managed to negotiate with some of the women cooking in the kitchen, persuading them to do scrambled eggs for at least one of the meals. However, a treat lay in store when an actor discovered she could buy tins of Beluga caviar from one of the male workers in the kitchen at a vastly reduced rate. She then sold it to her colleagues at a sizeable profit, thus nicely inflating her per diem allowance. The poor kitchen worker had muddled dollars and sterling to his disadvantage, but being unaware of his mistake, was delighted with his 'profit'.

On the company's first day off, a reception had been organised at the British Embassy in Moscow. Meanwhile, Thelma, Peter Hall and Alan Cohen, his Assistant Director, along with two or three of the leading actors, were invited to the house of Boris Vasiliev, the author of *Tomorrow Was War*, for a lunchtime gathering of the cast. We had become friendly with some of the young actors when this play was shown as part of our International 87 theatre season. One young actor, Anatoli, would become particularly close, visiting us in London only months later. Thelma, having discovered all her vodka disappearing ('including the miniatures I'd hidden at the back of the bathroom cupboard, Pealet!'), decided he was an alcoholic and arranged for him to go to an AA meeting. He returned flushed with excitement. 'Telma, just great fun at the club – I meet Anthony Hopkins!'

Vasiliev lived out in the countryside, so the party, unaware that travel from one zone to another was not permitted, made the journey illegally. Alan and the actors set off in one car while Thelma and Peter travelled in another. En route their car was stopped by the local police and they were promptly arrested. After protracted discussions employing her best Thelmaese, she managed to explain how important Sir Peter Hall was and that he had to catch a flight back to London later that afternoon. In the end, the police let them go, but only on condition they return immediately to Moscow. Thelma, for whom the thought of the lunch going on without her was not something she would ever contemplate, shouted at Peter that she was going to be sick if the car didn't stop. She got out and told the driver to continue on to Moscow with Peter as it was looking more and more likely he would miss his flight.

Thelma then sat in a ditch out of view and waited. Eventually, Anatoli – having realised when only one car arrived that something was wrong – came searching for her in his truck and took her off to the lunch party hidden behind the back seat.

Rosie, who was by this time beside herself with worry that Peter would miss his flight, had been trying to find the Stage Manager, Ernie, who had not returned with the others from the embassy reception. In fact, Ernie didn't go to the embassy, but had taken himself off to the National Hotel with a library book and ordered a couple of gin and tonics, with the intention of enjoying some peaceful time alone. The National Hotel had a bar, unlike the Peking, and was the only place that took currency other than roubles. It was therefore a favourite destination, and soon he was joined by other members of the cast and crew. After a while Ernie lost count of how many gin and tonics he had consumed.

When at last he reeled into the hotel he was fallen upon by a desperate Rosie, who had just been given some alarming news regarding Peter's whereabouts. As Ernie zigzagged unsteadily towards the lift, Rosie realised he was drunk and any discussion about Peter's impending flight would be pointless. Even so, as the lift doors opened she said to Ernie, 'Peter Hall's been arrested by the KGB!' at which point he burst out laughing and promptly collapsed flat on his face. As Rosie turned round to make her way back to the hotel lobby, Peter strolled in and on seeing her said calmly, 'Do you think you could get my luggage for me, darling?'

On the day the company was due to fly from Moscow to Tbilisi, a problem arose with Aeroflot. To begin with, there were not enough seats on the plane to accommodate everyone booked to fly. After hours of haggling, Thelma and Alan managed to get everyone on planes, except themselves. Rosie sat down on the last plane out that night and was unable to fasten her safety belt, to which the stewardess responded, 'On these planes it is much better not to wear your safety belt.' When the water she had asked for turned out to be a murky brown colour, she decided it was better not to touch that either. Thelma said flying with Aeroflot was like flying in something made of balsa wood and elastic bands.

After several hours at the airport trying to get herself and Alan onto a plane, she eventually resorted to phoning Raisa Gorbachev. Because of her relationship with Robert Sturua who ran the Rustaveli Theatre in Tbilisi, Thelma had considerable connections in Moscow. It was Robert's production of *Richard III* that she had brought from Georgia to the Roundhouse in 1979. A famous Georgian actor called Ramaz Chkhikvadze had played the title role and on the recce visit to Georgia his wife Natalia had given Thelma an enormous diamond that she had brought back into the country secreted about her person. Strings were pulled and they were booked on the first flight out to Tbilisi the following morning.

This meant spending another night in Moscow, and with only one room available at the hotel, they had to share. To their dismay, the room was infested with cockroaches, and while Alan stood on the bed screaming, Thelma in Boadicea mode went around the room stamping on them.

A day without a call from Thelma was always a day of disappointment for me. The clock continued to tick very slowly on the South Bank, while overseas it appeared they were in a *Carry On* film.

Indeed, a more serious problem was about to manifest itself. The trucks had three days to get from Moscow to Tbilisi in time to set up for the first performance. The company arrived in Tbilisi on a Monday, and by Thursday when the opening performance of *Cymbeline* was due to play, there was no sign of the sets or the costumes. Much speculation circulated: had the trucks been sabotaged and the contents seized?

Thelma had gone without sleep for days in her tireless pursuit of the lorries carrying our scenery and costumes. By Sunday, when all three productions were to play in one day, the company had performed the three plays on consecutive evenings with nothing but a few hastily assembled props. These included an old trunk, some swords which had seen better days, and John the Baptist's head on loan from the Opera House (where it is perhaps fortunate that a production of *Salome* was playing as we were also in need of a severed head). One of the design team was caught smuggling bed sheets out of his hotel room to use as a shroud for the corpse in *Cymbeline*, and to replace the tarpaulin under which Caliban and Trinculo hide in *The Tempest*. Steven

Mackintosh, who as Ariel was used to being flown onto stage and delivering his lines from an elevated position, calmly walked out on stage, while Geraldine James wore jeans and a sun hat (there was a heatwave in Tbilisi at the time).

The trucks finally arrived late on the Sunday, after the final performance. They had broken down north of the Georgian border, not through any mechanical failure but because the drivers had found twenty gallons of water in the diesel fuel. The drivers received a round of applause as they walked into the theatre.

# 13

## The Theory of Absolute Certainty

We spent many hours at Heathrow Airport over the years during which we hosted foreign companies at the National Theatre. One memorable occasion – and a good example of Thelma's theory of absolute certainty (or as Malcolm called it, 'The Gospel according to . . . ') – was when collecting the troupe from the Moscow Arts Theatre who were to perform *Uncle Vanya* with Innokenti Smoktunovsky as part of the second World Theatre Season in 1989.

We were standing in our usual position at Terminal 3 with huge numbers of other expectant people, and I found myself checking with Thelma that she would remember what the technicians looked like (they always came through before the actors). She assured me that of course she would as there was a marvellous-looking carpenter. 'Darling, if I was ten years younger . . .' Thelma always said that when she found a young man attractive; she likes young men.

One of the cliffhangers when meeting these large companies was that the coach we organised was only released from the coach park when the baggage was in the hall. So you could never check it was there in advance.

I would go and find a payphone and ring a surly man at the coach station, who would rarely be willing to confirm whether our coach was waiting. If they came through quickly and the coach had not been released, Thelma and I would have anything up to eighty very tired people standing with their baggage and, in the case of the Japanese, costumes, props, etc. in large trunks, outside the terminal. Actually only once in about ten years did the coach not materialise, and in this instance we put everyone in taxis and charged the coach firm.

People always stared at us. I am not sure whether it was to do with the often strange outfits Thelma selected – and who could blame her, since many of these pick-ups were so early in the morning that she and I would have to set our alarms for 4 or 5 a.m. in order to be there in time. Eventually a rather unusual-looking man in a brown suit and pale blue shirt with an odd-coloured tie, trousers that were far too short, baseball cap to one side, appeared and just stood in the exit lane from customs.

Thelma nudged me immediately – 'One of ours, darling. Look at him – looks like he's on day release.' She moved forward in her all-in-one Babygro suit, in-stantly attracting the attention of almost everyone at T3 Arrivals – they *both* looked as though they were on day release. She appeared to be having a conversation with him; she turned to me and shouted, 'Yes, darling, one of ours,' and returned. He, however, remained rooted to the spot. 'Why isn't he coming?' I asked. 'Because he's an idiot, darling.' Then to him, waving her arms: 'Come on, babycake!' (one of the many things she would call anyone whose name she couldn't remember: babycake, inch-worm, snorkweed, or just darling). He remained rooted. Everyone was now looking at us, and him. She went back over to him and had a more animated conversation before returning to me – 'He's not one of ours, darling.' There was no point asking her who she thought he was.

We continued waiting, and the next wave was led by a tall dark man with a beard. 'Ah – now here we are, darling. He's the carpenter I told you about.' She rushed forward, embracing him and he embraced her back and gestured to a few of those around him. There followed much shaking of hands and hugging. She brought them all over to me. 'This is Sweetpea and she will sort you all out; we have to wait for the others, but she will start taking you down to our coach soon.' She then disappeared and I was left with a small group of Russians and no interpreter. I managed to communicate and to almost everything I said they replied 'yes' and nodded enthusiastically.

When I had a group of about thirty people I started to explain via the attractive carpenter, who seemed to understand a little English, that I would take them to the coach now, and as soon as the actors were ready we would head for the Hilton and if any of them wanted to visit the theatre after that we would take them.

At this point it became clear that something was wrong. Thelma returned and introduced me to the actors. I kept trying to talk to her while smiling and shaking hands with somewhat sweaty palms, but she kept waving me off – she often did this when I was trying to tell her something important. Eventually I managed to explain to her that I didn't know who they were, but they weren't for us. 'Nonsense, darling, this is Sergei.' To the tall bearded man: 'Sergei, *da*?' '*Niet*,' he replied. She grabbed an actor who spoke both languages, then turned to me and said, 'They're on their way to Manchester, darling – they're fucking pathologists, they cut people up! Get rid of them.'

# 14

## *Sweetpea's Ailments*

Thursday, 29 October
White spot in throat
Cannot fully open mouth

Monday, 2 November
Stomach feels really funny

Wednesday, 11 November
No movement in small of back
Tingling feeling down legs
Pins and needles in feet
(later)
'My left tit is hurting.'

Friday, 13 November
'I have a strange feeling in the back of my left knee
and it's travelling up my left arm.'

Tuesday, 17 November
'I hope I'm not getting that pneumonia-type thing.'
'I'm terribly hot and Thelma keeps coughing on me.'

Friday, 20 November
'I have got such a pain in my coozie. It's like
someone is sticking a hot rod up there. I'm so
pre-menstrual.'

'I want to have a new, fresh doctor look at my foot.'
'My fanny feels like a pincushion.'

## Wednesday, 2 December

'I've got one of those tight tickly chests.'
(later)
'I've got such a tight, wheezy, hurty chest.'
(later still)
'I feel really fuzzy, blurred and out of focus.'
(and even later)
'If she's given me whooping cough there's going to be trouble!'

## Thursday, 3 December

'I feel a bit better in myself. My chest is my weak spot. I wonder if it's genetic?'

## Friday, 4 December

'I feel all achy.'

## Thursday, 10 December

'I've got such backache, just as if someone's put an iron rod in there.'

## Friday, 18 December

'I think I am developing asthma.'

## Monday, 22 February

'And I've got my third cold since Christmas.'
'I have a funny sensation when I eat a Mars Bar.'

## Wednesday, 24 February

'Will someone make my headache, which I have had all

day and all day yesterday, go away?'
Thelma: 'Yes, cut your head off!'

<u>Wednesday, 3 March</u>
'I keep getting funny pains in my head.'

<u>Thursday, 11 March</u>
'My eyes ache when I move them. Do you ever get
that?'

<u>Thursday, 18 March</u>
'I have such bad neuralgia today. I had it last night
in the lecture, but I was on camera and didn't dare
touch my head.'
'I hope I'm not getting something. I'll probably be
ill on my day off tomorrow.'

<u>Wednesday, 24 March</u>
'My teeth really hurt today.'

<u>Monday, 12 April</u>
'This sore throat came from nowhere — a kind of short
sharp infection.'

<u>Tuesday, 13 April</u>
'I want to feel better tomorrow, Jesus!'

<u>Wednesday, 14 April</u>
Off sick

<u>Friday, 23 April</u>
'I feel a bit sick today. I hope that meat was all
right last night.'

(the day she read an article about Arab habits with lamb)

Friday, 14 May
'It's very unpleasant. It's going down my legs now.'
(referring to backache, I think)

Monday, 17 May
'Do you think it was that biscuit? I've got the most terrible pain in my stomach.'

Thursday, 20 May
'The bit between my breasts is really tender. Do you ever get that? It feels bruised, as if I have been punched.'

Monday, 7 June
'I keep getting tingling sensations on my face. Do you think something has got trapped? Do you think something's caught up? Should I get worried about it? It's obviously connected to what is in my shoulder. It makes me think I have loads of hairs all over my face.'
(later)
'I've got a really funny feeling on the top of my head.'
(later still)
'Every time I swallow cold liquid it hurts.'

Tuesday, 8 June
'I think I've got your sore throat, or whoever started it.'

Wednesday, 9 June

'I feel sick all of a sudden.'

Vicky (receptionist): 'Have a chewing-gum.'


Monday, 14 June

'I just didn't sleep at all last night. Every time I lay on my back I felt sick.'

'You know how tummy ache can make you feel ill all over.'


Thursday, 17 June

'I've got weird toothache when I bite.'


Wednesday, 14 July

'I've got a terribly nervous chest. I feel as if something's going to burst out of it.'


Monday, 19 July

'I was about to drop off and my chest jumped.'


Tuesday, 20 July

'I'm terribly aware of my tongue all of a sudden.'


Wednesday, 21 July

'My arms are killing me. I think I've got arthritis.'


Monday, 16 August

'I've got a really funny feeling in the ends of my fingers. Do you ever get that — a sort of pins and needles, tingling feeling? I hope I'm not getting something.'

(later)

```
'I know it sounds silly, but wind can be really
debilitating.'
(Vicky: 'Oh tell me about it!')
```

```
Tuesday, 17 August
'That's typical, isn't it? I will probably be ill and
not have a holiday at all.'
```

The above are extracts from a record Malcolm kept
by covertly tapping into his computer whatever I said
that related to a health concern. This went on for over a
year before he gave it to me.

I don't know when I started being a hypochondriac.
At eighteen, I read *The White Album* by Joan Didion and
found strange comfort in the following lines retrieved
from her own psychiatric report: '*In June of this year
patient experienced an attack of vertigo, nausea, and a
feeling she was going to pass out. A thorough medical
evaluation elicited no positive findings . . .*'

In the early years with Thelma I had no idea how to
pace myself. I would burn on all cylinders and then not
burn at all. I put everything into it, worked weekends
and evenings when necessary – which it nearly always
was when we were presenting foreign work at the National Theatre – an eighteen-hour day was not unusual.

I didn't go on holiday because I didn't want to miss
anything. At the same time, I was trying to keep up with
my party-going friends, most of whom were students
and didn't have to get up in the morning and make
their way to responsible jobs. Sharing a flat with boys
who were busy taking a lot of drugs meant I was often
forced to behave like a martinet as I attempted to get
some sleep before another demanding day. This meant

emerging from my room at three o'clock in the morning to face a room full of people with dilated pupils, huddled round a bong. I'd have to scream that if the music wasn't turned off immediately I would throw them all out for good. They'd dissolve into fits of cannabis-induced giggles as I disappeared back into my room. Quite why I felt it necessary to creep around quietly at 7 a.m. the following morning I now see, with regret, was a missed opportunity to redress the balance.

Trying to impose any kind of order or keep the place remotely clean also threatened to make me middle-aged before my time. Washing up, for Charlie at least, was out of the question. Often when I came to cook there was an empty flat and a pile of dishes, so I'd have to wash up before I could start. This cycle was broken, albeit temporarily, when one night in desperation I took everything upstairs and laid it neatly on his bed – greasy plates, pans, frying pans, cutlery, and pulled the duvet over it. That night he came home with a date.

During a particularly busy time I returned home at midnight to a suspiciously quiet flat. I went to the kitchen to fetch a glass of water but couldn't open the door. I pushed and pushed, but it wouldn't budge. I gave up. The next day I discovered that the kitchen ceiling had fallen in and the entire kitchen was full of rubble. I just had to leave it and get to work. When I returned the following evening, nothing had been done about it.

Sometimes at the early morning meetings at the National Theatre, I would scan the boardroom table and note the impossibility of any of my colleagues having emerged from quite the same kind of chaos as I had. My domestic and professional lives were at complete odds.

These conditions only fuelled my hypochondria. Whatever the talked-of disease was at the time, I thought I had it. When I was twenty-three I awoke in the early hours with a pain in my left breast, sat up in bed and put my hand straight on a lump. A little lump the size of a pea. Panic. I imagined the worse. I telephoned my mother, who told me to go to the doctor the following morning, but assured me that as it hurt it was probably fine. My doctor sent me to St Mary's Hospital where I saw a wonderful surgeon who did a drawing on my breast and said that under anaesthetic she would push the lump up and out under my nipple so that I would not have an obvious scar.

I hated not being at work, but was not allowed back for two days after the operation. I returned with a large pad, rather like a sanitary towel, strapped to my breast. I had no feelings of embarrassment about this, I just loved being back. The trouble began when the wound wouldn't heal. Thelma and I were working at the National one afternoon; I was typing and she was talking, non-stop as usual. I felt something warm and wet running down onto my stomach. 'I'm bleeding,' I said. 'Just finish this, darling, we're nearly done, and then I'll get you a minicab to the hospital.' We did finish, by which time there was blood all over my clothes. Short of losing consciousness, Thelma really didn't take indisposition of any kind at all seriously.

# 15

## *Chrysanthemum*

During the second visit by the Japanese company in 1989, one of the young Japanese actors scaled the outside of the Hilton Hotel in Kensington. He had mislaid his key and a point of honour required this act of bravery rather than simply asking the desk for a replacement key. He fell from the second floor and broke both feet.

He was in disgrace at St Mary's Hospital, Paddington. The Japanese disowned him and he was there for three weeks before his parents were summoned from Tokyo to take him home.

Thelma went to see him immediately and told him that she would send me to visit: a prospect that apparently delighted him. The next morning I made the short walk to St Mary's Hospital armed with a box of Terry's All Gold, a National Theatre T-shirt, and a card signed by the crew. Thelma told me he was in the Joseph Toynbee Ward on the second floor. When I said I couldn't remember which of the actors he was (there were eighty-eight of them) she assured me that I did – he was the one we had nicknamed 'Chrysanthemum' on account of his amazing hair. 'Anyway, darling,' she said, 'you can't miss him, he's the only Japanese man on the ward.'

I arrived at the Joseph Toynbee, announced myself, and was told he had been moved to a room on his own.

He was having a scan, but I was welcome to go and wait in his room. It was quite stuffy and the sun beat in through the unopened south-facing windows. There were a lot of cards, but otherwise no clues. I waited. About fifteen minutes later a doctor pushed a wheelchair towards me in which sat a Japanese man I didn't recognise, but who did look very in the mode of Ninagawa. Crucially, he was wearing two enormous black boots over casts on his feet. Alarmingly his head was shaved, but I didn't think this too peculiar. What did trouble me were the drips and various things sticking into his wrists.

'HELLLO-O-O,' I said, enunciating clearly as he spoke little English. 'I – AM – SWEETPEA – FROM – THE – NATIONAL – THEATRE.' (Typical Thelma, I thought, he doesn't know who the hell I am.)

'Aaahhhh,' he said, bowing low in his wheelchair. 'National Theatre, aaahhhh.'

'Yes,' I continued. 'I have brought you chocolates' – offering up the gold box.

'Aaahhh, sank you.'

'And,' I said, unravelling and offering up the T-shirt, 'this.'

'Aaaahhhhhh, National Theatre . . . aaaaaahhhhh!'

'And here is a card from everyone to say get well soon – how are you feeling?'

'Ahhh, not so bad, feet mending, but hepatitis makes me feel not so good . . . '

HEPATITIS! Jesus, I thought – get me out of this tiny disease-filled room! Running through my head at this point was the terrifying notion that since Thelma had been the day before, he'd developed this terrible condition and had been moved to a single room so as not to infect the entire ward. I hastily finished my speech – trying not to breathe in too much – while backing out of the door. 'Thelma is coming to see you later with a take-away from Ajimura,' I said. I left him looking stunned and repeating his 'sank you's' and the words 'National Theatre'.

I jumped on a 23 bus outside the hospital that took me all the way to the office and during the journey managed to convince myself that I was going to be very ill. I even started to *feel* very ill. I was furious by the time I got back, stomping into the office like a petulant child and sitting down at my desk.

Thelma finished her phone call and was impatient to hear about our friend. 'Well, darling, how was he?'

'How could you!' I said. 'He's in a room on his own! He's got hepatitis!'

Malcolm spat his coffee out and Thelma roared with laughter.

'Darling, come and sit here and tell me exactly which son of Nippon you gave your chocolates to.'

She later told Ninagawa, his producer Tadao Nakane, and Peter Hall that this man must have thought I was on day release, a young blonde brandishing chocolates and a T-shirt and saying that someone called Thelma would be bringing food from Ajimura. The story was then repeated in full to the entire Japanese company, who at the end stood and clapped. I was a genuine idiot, but unlike our poor friend Chrysanthemum, somewhere else in the hospital still waiting for Sweetpea and her chocolates, I was not in disgrace.

# 16

## *Dustin Hoffman's Dressing Gown*

There's only ever been one other Sweetpea in Thelma's life, and that was just briefly. In 1989 Dustin Hoffman came to London to play Shylock in Peter Hall's production of *The Merchant of Venice*. Discussions between Duncan Weldon, Peter Hall and Thelma about forming the Peter Hall Company had begun while we were still working at the National. Peter was due to leave his post there as Director and we would cross the river with him. Thelma was to be Executive Producer, Peter the talent, and Duncan would finance it all.

There had been no sad farewell parties when we left the National – we weren't entirely leaving. Richard Eyre wanted to continue with the foreign theatre visits, so Thelma remained as Head of International Theatre and an office was always made available to us. This was good news; although excited about our future, I was also sad to be leaving the National.

On the first day of rehearsals for *The Merchant of Venice*, Thelma shouted for me across a crowded rehearsal room. I didn't hear her – I was making tea and coffee for nervous actors. Dustin came up and stood in front of her.

'You called?' he said.

'Not you, darling, I called Sweetpea.'

'I am Sweetpea,' he replied.

'Well, you are Sweetpea number two, because there's a number one already – she's over there.'

I was summoned and introduced by Thelma to the other Sweetpea. 'Pea darling, this is Sweetpea Hoffman.' It transpired that this had been his nickname since babyhood because he used to crawl up everything. So this was how Dustin and I bonded and became the two Sweetpeas.

Duncan had not initially realised that saying yes to Thelma – whom Peter was insisting upon – meant also saying yes to her entourage: Malcolm and me. Duncan had his own large organisation, and as he saw it they were perfectly capable of dealing with the workload. Having made it very clear what he wanted, Peter withdrew from the fray, leaving Thelma and Duncan to hammer out the details.

The Peter Hall Company existed in name only, being in effect under the umbrella of Duncan's organisation. His offices were located in Waldorf Chambers next door to the Waldorf Hotel, and he had secured offices for the Peter Hall Company just around the corner in Exeter Street.

This was the smartest office space we ever shared, with the three of us in one huge room with many more windows than we were used to at the National. Peter occupied newly furnished rooms adjacent to ours behind louvred doors. Thelma never learnt how to use the new telephone system; regularly omitting to press the right button for an outside line, she was often well into a monologue before our receptionist was brave enough to interrupt her.

Thelma kept telling me we were now working in

'the commercial sector' not 'the subsidised sector'. But though she had stepped out of the subsidised world, her subsidised mentality prevailed. Whether taxpayers' money or someone else's, she was always very prudent financially.

Having won his second Oscar for *Rain Man*, Dustin was about as famous as it was possible to be by the time he arrived in London for rehearsals. He lived in Kensington with no entourage other than a PA employed to look after things while he was in London. He enjoyed walking to the rehearsal room in Chelsea and often all the way to our offices in Exeter Street. Sometimes he would take me to one side in the office in order to listen to him learning his lines. Though I didn't consider myself starstruck, I could hardly believe that I was sitting with the man my brother and I had grown up watching in films like *The Graduate* and *Midnight Cowboy*.

Dustin was very likeable and unstarry, in the way that truly major actors often are. He was charismatic, funny and mischievous, but above all a great actor, and I felt privileged to witness him at work. At twenty-three, though, I still wasn't confident enough to express my opinions in the company of professionals like Dustin Hoffman or Peter Hall.

As we walked up Holborn with the pair of them to have lunch in a pub near the rehearsal room, people were stopping dead in their tracks when they realised who the small animated man was. It seemed ordinary in the sense that I was merely having lunch with my colleagues, but at the same time extraordinary. This was probably one of the first times I had been to a lunch without Thelma and I cannot remember why that happened. But later, when we got back to the rehearsal room, Dustin asked if I would stay and watch some rehearsals. I rang the office to ask permission, but Thelma summoned me back. Apparently it would not have been appropriate. I didn't think too much of it at the time, except that I was of course a little disappointed. Retrospectively I felt robbed of a defining moment.

An American star on the London stage was at this time still a novelty, it had not become the trend it would a decade later both in the West End and at the Donmar Warehouse. As the run was sold out, Thelma organised a few seats for our nearest and dearest at our first public preview. Hodie arrived partially dressed in a pair of Bondi Beach surf shorts, flip-flops and a vivid flower-print shirt unbuttoned halfway down his chest. By the time we had taken our seats in the dress circle, I realised he was absolutely dripping with sweat. During the play he clutched my hand, holding on tightly and repeating 'sorry' in my ear. I discovered later that he was having a massive trip after he and a friend had been dropping acid in Hyde Park all day. Once again my two worlds were colliding.

But for me the highlight was introducing Hodie to Dustin at the first-night party in London, watching him shake hands with the Graduate. I staggered about in three-inch orange heels and an old 1930s apricot-coloured dress. Thelma had purchased these for me at a Christie's sale of Mrs Chrysler's wardrobe – she'd had to buy the entire lot in order to get a particular dress: a beautiful beaded strappy cocktail number. I was six feet tall in those shoes and immensely uncomfortable. Because Duncan had organised the party and not us, there was proper grand food – lobster! Hodie and our friend

Oliver had dressed as smartly as they could in old suits, odd shirts and ties, and Doc Marten shoes. I didn't get to eat any food. As we left, Oliver was mistaken for Rupert Graves by the assembled photographers, and they ran ahead, leaving me to totter painfully behind them.

Dustin's first-night gift to us all was a dressing gown with *The Merchant of Venice* embroidered on the back and our initials embossed on the front. They were very good quality, I still have mine and suspect there are a few more hanging on the backs of bathroom doors in London.

I put the headaches, backache and leg ache down to hard work and bad posture – my office chair was threadbare and fit only for a munchkin. There was no money for swanky chairs. I pointed out to Thelma that Peter Hall's assistant had a special chair for people with back problems: 'The chair is ridiculous, darling, she looks as if she's kneeling.' But when a couple of friends independently asked me why I was limping, I made an appointment to see an osteopath.

I lay flat on the examining table, he pulled my legs and measured and pulled again. 'Well, you've got long legs, young lady, and one that's even longer than the other!' A difference of 1.5 centimetres is enough for them to take notice and I was offered a shoe lift. This was a blow. No more sandals, flip-flops or espadrilles, and certainly Mrs Chrysler's shoes were now out of the question. My lift was to significantly limit the range of footwear choices, unless I had the sole of the shoe enhanced, though this wasn't available on the National Health. When I arrived back at the office Thelma laughed, saying I reminded her of Laura in *The Glass*

*Menagerie*. I thought to myself that a shoe lift was not quite as dramatic as a calliper. 'Darling, the child's got one leg longer than the other,' I'd hear her say with glee to pretty much anyone who called that day.

*Merchant* was a huge success, and transferred to Broadway after the London run. With all our work completed, Thelma managed to get Malcolm and me to New York for the opening night. A limousine was laid on to take us from the airport to Manhattan, and I had the distinct feeling of being like a character in one of the many noir movies I watched as a teenager. Added to which, never having stayed in a hotel anywhere before, our modest version was a sumptuous and completely novel experience. A trouser press, a hitherto unknown object, appeared as a bizarre device out of a Surrealist painting, while the luxury tea-making facility and television were equally novel.

The opening was in the week before Christmas and, unprepared for the city's freezing temperatures, I stood shivering outside the theatre in a flimsy borrowed silk dress crumpled beneath my black woollen coat, which proved wholly inadequate protection against a New York winter night.

The after-show party was a grand, starry event, so having travelled far and eaten little, the champagne went straight to my head. Soon after this I was introduced to what I thought was a mirage, which then spoke to me in a growling, familiar tone – 'What's a nice kid like you doing in a shit city like this at Christmas?' Lauren Bacall patted her knees, offering me a seat on her lap.

The magic of the evening was complete.

# 17

## *West End Girl*

Ah, but I was so much older then,
I'm younger than that now.

Bob Dylan

Just around the corner from our office, youth culture was exploding in Soho. Friends were busy popping Ecstasy and clubbing. On a Friday evening people would gather in the flat and bang tequila slammers on an old black briefcase before heading for the clubs. Meanwhile, I would be on my way to a theatre to spend the evening with people twice my age, sitting in old Italian restaurants staring at walls lined with photographs signed by the famous. On the odd occasion I joined them at a club, but rarely lasted more than an hour, being a hopeless dancer – all arms and legs, and without drugs, extremely self-conscious. I'd wander back through Leicester Square with the music reverberating in my chest like another heartbeat.

I was too scared to take Ecstasy, cocaine, or indeed anything else. Convinced I would have a heart attack, and wired enough as it was, my drug of choice was the theatre. When a friend described the effects of Ecstasy, I realised that the heightened reality and clarity were similar to what I experienced as an unexpectedly natural high when watching something like *The Hairy Ape*.

My flatmates and our friends seemed to think that I didn't know how to enjoy myself. 'Don't pick up!' I'd screech, as a famous voice would boom into the room inviting me to Sunday lunch. The assembled company would sit in wide-eyed amazement that I didn't want to go. 'But it's so and so!' I explained that if I accepted I would only be standing at a sink peeling potatoes or pouring people wine – not necessarily my idea of a fun day off.

The weight of responsibility for the flat, making sure there was enough money in the company account to pay the bills and that we got the lease extended for another year, fell entirely on my shoulders. On discovering that Fifi's boyfriend was growing 'grass' in our roofspace, I was furious – and anxious – because Mr Heap (the plumber employed by the landlords) could have found it on one of his many visits to the water tank, and it was my name on the contract. Although unsure if it was the same boyfriend who wrapped the fridge in cling film, I was usually the unsuspecting victim of such pranks and rarely saw the funny side.

Fifi was mortified and clearly oblivious to what he was doing. I didn't like the boyfriend, especially as he would use my towel and made it obvious that he thought me uptight. What most of the men passing through the flat considered uptight behaviour was as follows:

1. Not wanting to get drunk on Sunday evening; not wanting to share their drugs;
2. Getting angry because someone had upended a large yucca plant and left the soil all over the carpet; or when someone had not removed broken glass on the stairs;
3. Being bothered when they failed to flush the loo after going big ways;

4. Eating my food.

Food was a big thing in the flat. It was not unusual, for example, to come home and find dishes of food everywhere, covered in cling film. A note from Fifi apologising for the fact she'd had to use every available receptacle (she'd got another cooking job). There were frequent messages on the answer machine from clients asking for things like lobster, organic butter – 'the butter must be organic' – and lemon tart. The lemon tart caused Fifi considerable stress. Apparently there is a degree of alchemy involved in making a good lemon tart.

It was always good news for us when Fifi had another cooking commission because we were treated to wonderful leftovers. One of our friends who lived down the road and who was out of work used to come home to find packets of cheese and bags of rocket posted through his letter box. Neither was it unusual to come home and find the kitchen full of boxes of peppers, courgettes and aubergines. Charlie had been to Portobello at the end of the afternoon on his way home from college and bought things going cheap. We ate ratatouille for days afterwards. Occasionally I joined in the cooking frenzies at weekends, but Hodie and Charlie were a formidable team and usually my role was general factotum. We invariably had lots of people coming for supper; the flat was big enough and rough around the edges enough to engender a very relaxed environment. Too relaxed for me, sometimes; the chaos could be unsettling when viewed from my work perspective.

I did my best to keep parties away from the flat, but occasionally had to relent. Usually, having drunk too much by about 10 p.m., which is when it seemed most people started to arrive, I would lock myself in my room. But as this was on the same floor as the party, sleep was impossible and so was access to the bathroom, so I'd have to pee in the sink in my room. I would fret about being fit for work, I would fret about the mess. The noise would go on until 4 or 5 a.m., at which point the door would slam, serially. In the morning I would pick my way through bodies, bottles, overflowing ashtrays and head for the bathroom, often to find more bodies there – total strangers. Charlie had put a sign up at college advertising the party. When Harry downstairs did the same thing, I came across her squeezing through the throng with a black bin liner, collecting all the discarded cans and bottles. 'Sweetpea – I don't know who *any* of these people are!' The following morning I found her on the doorstep wearing a pair of Marigolds, picking up a turd.

Our kitchen buzzed on a Saturday afternoon as we prepared supper for friends. Music played loudly from the record player in my bedroom. They played 'Hey Joe' so many times I never wanted to hear Jimi Hendrix again. I was in charge of making the 'boiled Moroccan carrot salad', a task assigned to me with some reluctance by Hodie. I was working on the draining board as they had taken up all available work surfaces. The window was open and a gentle summer breeze wafted in as I piled ingredients into the food processor. As I added the juice of two lemons, Hodie, carrying a tray of garlic bread aloft, said, 'What are you doing?!' I replied with weary certainty, 'I'm adding the juice of two lemons.' Grabbing the book, he snapped, 'There are no lemons in the recipe.' The pages had been turning over in the breeze and I was halfway through a recipe for a lemon tart.

# 18

## *Porridge with Richard Harris*

'He's gone,' I said to Thelma quietly. *He* was the second director hired for Richard Harris in Pirandello's *Henry IV*. She waved me away. She was on the phone to California, discussing the casting of our next production. I'd witnessed the director in a heated conversation with Richard, who kicked a filing cabinet and swore at him. The director grabbed his bag and stormed out. When Thelma hung up I said again, 'Thelma – he's gone.' To which she replied, 'Don't worry, darling, I'll see him tomorrow.' 'No,' I said, 'I think he's walked out!' She laughed, and then widened her eyes and opened her mouth in amazement.

Thelma always did this when there was the whiff of 'meringue'-style trouble. Serious trouble was something else. But this 'meringue' kind of trouble she rode with surety. She had an innate confidence about such things. It was almost thrilling, and in truth was the kind of problem she loved solving. We had no director and were due to start rehearsing in little over two weeks, and if we could not replace him in that time the production would be cancelled.

In fact, we got through another three before the opening night in London. In addition, we would work our way through three sets of translators, three designers, two casting directors, two productions managers. We would also cancel three previews, three press nights and lose two theatres, eventually opening at Wyndham's Theatre on 23 May 1990. Finally, we parted company with Sarah Miles for a second time.

While preparing for this we were of course still working with Peter Hall, whose production of *The Wild Duck* (or as we called it, 'The Flying Fuck') had just begun rehearsals. We were also planning more foreign work at the National, as well as a transfer of *Bent* with Ian McKellen from the National to the West End.

As if all this wasn't enough, Thelma was also due to go to Romania, a trip we were organising with the British Council. This would require passport photographs, and as we were due to work at the National Theatre that afternoon, we left our office in Exeter Street to find a taxi to Waterloo Station, where in those days there was a photo booth. It was pouring with rain and we were drenched within minutes and running late for a planned lunch with an associate at the NT to discuss foreign work and the possibility we would continue to present it at the National. I hailed a cab and as we reached it a man appeared from nowhere, opened the door and hopped in.

Just then, a voice behind us boomed out, 'Not in front of the Waldorf, madam! Not in front of the Waldorf!'

Neither of us had noticed the doorman there in his dark green Waldorf uniform, holding a large umbrella. He was not looking pleased.

Thelma said very calmly, 'I'm very sorry, we didn't see you . . .'

But before she could say more he went on, 'This is Waldorf territory, this is my patch! Not on my patch!' We were now back in front of the Waldorf.

'I always get my cabs here, our office is just there,' said Thelma, pointing vaguely behind her. 'There really is no need to be so rude.'

'I'm not being rude!' he replied, by now bright red in the face.

'Well, I think you are, and if you continue to talk to me in this manner I will have to ask to speak with your superior.'

Eyes bulging, he retorted, 'Madam! You have no etiquette!'

At this point, Thelma suddenly dispensed with the grown-up image, adopted her childlike squeak (rather reminiscent of Miranda Richardson as Queen Elizabeth I in *Blackadder*), and began jumping up and down on the spot.

'Can you spell it, can you spell it?'

I thought he was going to hit her, so grabbing her arm I steered her towards the Strand.

'You shouldn't use words you can't spell!' she squeaked, over her shoulder.

By the time we reached the photo booth we were running late, and in her impatience Thelma, who was unable to grasp the instructions, kept pressing the wrong button and couldn't get the seat at the right height. 'Just sit still, look straight ahead and wait for the green light!' I said. Eventually I thought we'd got it right. It took an interminable five minutes for the photographs to emerge, with Thelma hitting the machine and poking her fingers into the slot the whole time. When the photo dropped out we stood looking at it. 'What *were* you doing?' I said, contemplating her image with its vacant expression, the wandering eyes that seemed to be searching heavenwards. 'I was looking for the green light, darling.'

That afternoon we were supposed to be working at the National, preparing another season of foreign visits. The phone started ringing and the Richard Harris problems once more took priority. *Henry IV* was due to start in Bradford, but Richard refused to open there. He had been unhappy with the director, in particular with the names of actors he was coming up with – none of whom any of us had heard of. Richard's shambolic mien belied his attention to detail and a steely determination to get what he wanted. Meanwhile, Sarah Miles's agent was fighting for her to receive more money. The management was adamant that this would not be so. It was, in this instance, easy for Thelma to stick to her guns; she didn't care if Sarah said no. By the end of that particular afternoon, Thelma had persuaded Richard to open in Bradford, and Sarah Miles's agent had accepted the management's offer.

Richard Harris was high-maintenance. Thelma loved him for his brilliance as an actor – she found his work on stage very exciting – but also because he was Irish and ate porridge, as she herself did. Richard no longer drank, and appeared to *live on* porridge; this was certainly what he ate most nights in his dressing room before going on stage. The porridge settled his stomach, which was often upset by nerves, and he ate it with a silver spoon with his initials on, a present from Thelma.

Richard was tall and still looked strong, but his face was always pasty, and creased with the years. Thelma told him one evening that he looked like 'a half-baked apple strudel'. They had a robust, playful relationship and he became considerably reliant on her regular dressing room visits. I was usually with her, and he trusted me by the time we opened in the West End.

I had been around on the fateful night in Cardiff when he had locked himself in his dressing room, refusing to come out or to go on stage for that evening's performance. Duncan Weldon, having been unable to reason with him, eventually summoned Thelma. She knocked on the door and pleaded with Richard to let her in, at which the door opened a fraction and an arm came out and pulled her in. I waited outside. Richard wanted the understudy to go on that night and he would go on the following night. 'No, you won't,' said Thelma. 'If you don't go on tonight you will not go on for the rest of the tour and by the time we get to London we will have found someone who won't be a tenth of you, but we *will* replace you.' It was at this point that she gave him her most treasured rosary beads. Then the door opened and I was allowed into the inner sanctum. After the performance, Duncan Weldon took us all to dinner where Richard announced he wanted Director Number Three fired.

By the time the production reached the next venue, it was clear that he and Sarah Miles were not a marriage made in heaven. Richard believed there was no electricity between them on stage. Later, as Thelma entered her dressing room to discuss the situation with her, Sarah said, 'Here comes the angel of death.'

Only once during the run in London did I have to visit Richard's dressing room alone. Despite Thelma having warned him of her impending absence, by the time I knocked on his dressing room door he had clearly forgotten and seeing me alone bellowed, 'Where's that fucking Irish red-headed bitch!' (He always referred to her as Irish, despite the fact it was Thelma's mother who was born in Dunmanway, not her. 'No, no, you were born in Dunmanway,' he would insist. 'How did you lose your accent?')

I couldn't tell if he was joking or not, but before I could explain where she was he had picked me up and thrown me across the dressing room on to a divan in front of the wall, which I narrowly missed smashing my head against. This was his idea of being friendly. I composed myself, then had to sit chatting to Richard, who sat crossed-legged on the divan opposite, oblivious to the fact that he had no pants on.

Thelma never got her rosary back.

Meanwhile, tensions were mounting between Thelma and Peter Hall. Much as he recognised Thelma's incomparable powers and how they served him, small things began to rankle, such as the idea of billing for Malcolm and me in the programme – we were due to be listed along with everyone else under 'For the Peter Hall Company . . . ' As we were not actually employed by the Peter Hall Company, Thelma wanted us listed under her name – for Thelma Holt Ltd. Peter finally conceded, but all this was just adding to a general distancing and disillusionment on our part, and although the moment of tension was short-lived, the timing could not have been worse. The call from Peter telling Thelma that we would have to move out of the offices in Exeter Street was a terrible shock.

As we left the National Theatre that evening, Thelma said, 'The only way to survive in this profession without becoming a manic depressive is to exercise huge amounts of self-deception.' I wondered if it got better or worse; she assured me the latter, but I would become better at dealing with it.

Thelma's ability to delude herself was masterful, and her ego robust enough to accommodate almost anything. She would continue to support Peter, praising his talents and the qualities she found admirable; they'd known each other since Thelma was twenty-two, and the friendship endured. I admired Thelma's single-mindedness, her unwavering belief in her own power. I never doubted her opinions and imagined everyone to be two steps behind her. We might be homeless, but Thelma's goose was about to lay a very golden egg and I believed I had the best job in the world.

But I was also struggling at work. Each month I would spend a good chunk of the day or night crouched on the bathroom floor, panting and drenched in sweat. I had learnt that it was best not to wait for the pain to get too settled in before popping painkillers – otherwise nothing seemed to touch it.

When the months of discomfort, sometimes considerable pain, and the general state of feeling unwell had become years, during which time I had made many visits to the GP, and sometimes Casualty – most memorably the occasion a doctor decided it was necessary to stick his hand up my bottom as I might have a twisted gut – my mother booked and paid for an appointment at the Marie Stopes Clinic.

Within ten minutes of describing my symptoms, the rather formidable female doctor told me it was most likely that I had endometriosis, but that a scan would confirm this. She did a drawing and explained what this condition was, and the room swam as I plucked up the courage to ask her if this was something I could die of. She told me in the next breath that it was unlikely I would be able to have children. At twenty-four I had not considered motherhood, and although fairly confident I didn't want it badly enough, I felt deeply upset about my brokenness. She sent me straight down to the Portland Hospital for a scan; my mouth dried at the thought of the costs, but fear about what was going on with my ovaries and my womb rather outweighed fiscal concerns. She told me that surgery could be booked almost immediately, and I tried to look normal when she told me how much this would cost.

At the Portland I wrote a cheque for £65 and the scan confirmed her diagnosis – and furthermore, the existence of two large endometrial cysts, the size of small oranges, on each of my ovaries. My parents offered to pay for the surgery, but I didn't want this and got myself into the NHS system. As it turned out, I wouldn't have to wait more than a month for surgery. Thelma, who had also never heard of endometriosis, brushed all this aside with her customary indifference. A couple of days later she told me delightedly that Marilyn Monroe had it. 'Look what happened to her, darling!' she guffawed.

My surgery was booked and I was told to take six weeks off work. This was clearly a bit of a blow to Thelma – 'We'll manage, darling.' The day before I was admitted she came round to Westbourne Terrace with a hand mirror and an antique nightdress. 'Darling, the worst thing about being in hospital is not being able to see yourself.' During the five weeks prior to surgery I had been put on a drug which shut down my cycle entirely, but which also made me look about six months pregnant. I couldn't do up any of my trousers, and sometimes I'd sit at my desk, trousers undone, with a hot water bottle to ease the cramping pains. 'What's wrong with the child?' I would hear Thelma enquire of Malcolm as I left the room. I dreaded the surgery, I was convinced I wouldn't wake up from the general anaesthetic. The time off work was also an anxiety – I didn't want to be off work and miss all that time in what Thelma called 'the fun factory'.

As I sat on the hospital bed in my gown, waiting to be taken to the operating theatre, the doctor arrived and told me that my most recent scan showed that the cysts had shrunk considerably, so they wanted to continue drug therapy and avoid surgery.

I was over the moon, and blissfully unaware that, as far as the endometriosis was concerned, this was just the beginning of a wrong turn on a very long road.

# 19

## *The House Full Sign Is Up*

Not long after Peter Hall had made us homeless, we moved into a tiny room at the very top of a building in Catherine Street, just up from the Duchess Theatre. From here we would mount the first production as Thelma Holt Ltd', *Three Sisters*.

Thelma wanted to form her very own company, to be creatively and financially independent. Her wish was to produce star-led revivals of classic plays in the West End and also to tour the regions. This meant forming a company and finding her own investors. To produce in the West End and therefore secure a theatre you had to be a member of what was then called the Society of West End Theatres (SWET) and is now called the Society of London Theatres (SOLT). Otherwise, one had to either come up with a large deposit or co-produce with someone who was a member. But Thelma wanted the freedom to choose her own plays, make her own choices. She didn't want to be answerable to anyone else, either financially or artistically.

She had been in discussion with Vanessa Redgrave about doing a play with her and two other members of the Redgrave family, her sister Lynn and daughter Joely. It was during a trip to America to discuss plans further with both Lynn and Vanessa, that the late Christopher Reeve (or Superman as Thelma always referred to him) suggested to Thelma that the perfect play for them all would be *Three Sisters*. In order to do this, she borrowed the money against the value of her house.

Looking back, I am not quite sure how we did it. The room was extremely small; we had two old electric typewriters and a couple of desks. Thelma had an old upright leather chair, but no desk. We shared a photo-copier and a kettle with the office below. There was no room for filing cabinets, so Malcolm had everything neatly stored in archive boxes, and at one point, before a second desk was found, I worked with a typewriter perched on top of the boxes, which I straddled. This office set-up, though eccentric, would continue even when we moved to larger offices with proper furniture. Thelma liked the three of us in one room so that we all knew everything. She originated this practice at home, where all the doors had been removed because she said, 'Cats don't like doors', and her beloved Siamese Shiva would have torn the doors to pieces.

Malcolm was always tidy and organised. At the end of every day, no matter how chaotic it had been, he would put the plastic cover on his typewriter, and later his computer, line up his pencils and shorthand notebooks and have his in-tray in order ready for the following morning. I never saw Malcolm (Mal, as Thelma and I called him) caught out. He was the sharpest person I'd ever met and without him I don't believe Thelma Holt Ltd would have functioned at all.

But whatever our future successes, we never expanded. Thelma maintained that some producers who had 'inhaled a success' and got over-ambitious had not long afterwards gone out of business. We didn't earn much between us, and if a production was doing badly, Thelma would stop drawing a salary.

We worked well as a team, with an efficient system and a division of tasks at its core. Thelma and Malcolm would put together all the financial elements, including the investors' documents and budgets. I would collate all the casting. The rest of the work would be shared and between us we would take care of every aspect and detail of mounting the production.

At this time the notion of a foreign director working with English actors was still relatively untried, certainly in the commercial sector. Thelma's choice of Robert Sturua was inspired by their collaboration on *Richard III* during her Roundhouse days. Communication with Tbilisi was challenging. There was no email, so we relied on a fax machine at the Rustaveli and the telephone, which was not easy because though he spoke a little English, it was not good enough for any detailed conversation.

The key in all this was Helen Molchanoff, who understood how to speak to actors and creative people (her father was the actor Richard Marner, who played Colonel Kurt Von Strohm in *'Allo 'Allo!*). Her understanding of our particular world and ability to 'interpret' within the interpreting was to prove invaluable. We had to bring Robert over to London on several occasions before rehearsals began in order to meet and audition actors. Robert reminded me of Fred, the spherical little man on the Mother's Pride flour packets. My relationship with him was always rather second-hand – everything was done via Helen. So perhaps I only knew Helen's version of Robert, which was a very mischievous, shrewd and likeable one. Helen looked a lot like her father and was incredibly funny and bright. Her skills at interpreting extended to the inner workings of her English colleagues and she and I would often exchange knowing glances as we both recognised inauthentic moments, or another of Thelma's crafty plots.

This was the first production on which Thelma put me in charge of casting; she believed I had a talent for it. However, I relied heavily on the advice of one or two favourite casting directors who were very generous with their opinions. I had neither the time nor the money to be at the theatre as often as was necessary in order to keep up with emerging talent. It was easy to cast well-known actors who had a reputation in the theatre, but casting younger actors or those whose work we might only have seen on television or film required the knowledge of someone who had seen them live on stage. Before letting Robert return to Tbilisi, we would make sure we had his number one, two and three choices of actor for each role so that we could move quickly if number one declined our offer. As names meant nothing to him, we would lay out on the floor 10-by-8 black-and-white photographs of the actors and label them by character name – he would take a duplicate set home with him.

The excitement around this production from early on was manifest in the very high calibre of actors we had coming to audition for Robert, for which purpose we hired the Strand Theatre for a week. It was protocol when casting actors who were famous or well known for them to come for a coffee to 'talk about the play'. Actors who were not stars but who were on the rise might be asked to read informally, and unknowns would read on stage so that we knew they could actually be heard at the back of the stalls, or 'project' as Thelma called it.

Because Robert was foreign and knew nobody, these procedures had to be handled delicately. We would explain to a famous actor's agent that the director might ask their client to read a little. This was a given and big names were happy to sit in the stalls chatting and reading, some would even offer to jump on stage. The key being we didn't ask it of them, rather let it unfold naturally during the meeting. Phoebe Nicholls, who played Natasha, initially refused to read for him, but was coaxed into coming back and was the most impressive Natasha I've ever seen. Her interpretation was stunning in its simplicity, conveying everything about how manipulative her character had become. I still remember to this day the obnoxious way she delivered the line, 'What's that fork doing here?' Casting this production was exciting and easy and we seemed spoilt for choice; in future this would not always be the case.

The investors had been secured and were no doubt impressed with the starry familial casting combination. It was a worry, therefore, when Joely Richardson had to pull out unexpectedly. Thelma fell out with Joely's agent, Michael Foster, but this froideur was short-lived and a couple of years later we cast his client Janet McTeer as Beatrice in *Much Ado About Nothing* and later in our award-winning *A Doll's House*. Despite the blow, we were still able to keep it in the family as Jemma Redgrave, Vanessa and Lynn's niece, took over as Irina.

When there was a problem, Thelma became unshakeable. The greater the problem, the more determined her resolution to solve it. Getting on the phone and talking things through, in her inimitable way, would shift perceptions and allow new opportunities to present themselves.

'Darling, get me Jimmy Sharkey' (Vanessa's agent in those days), 'Darling, get me Dickie Attenborough' – Thelma rarely dialled a call herself. Malcolm or I would pick up and dial, and so before long we had most, if not all in his case, the regular numbers in our heads. When very busy or fraught we would rebel and she would have to dial herself. Malcolm typed out a list of the regular names and numbers, blew them up on the photocopier and stuck them on the wall by her phone. This still meant interruption, as Malcolm would shout the number out while she dialled. Often misheard, his voice would rise to a shout as he repeated it for the third time. 'Is he there, darling?' she would say to an unsuspecting secretary. We would then hear Thelma say, 'Darling, it's me!' Depending upon the bravery of the person who had answered, 'me' would be put through, or we would hear her say in a flabbergasted tone, 'Thelma! It's Thelma!'

Despite the apparent armour-plating, Thelma did sometimes feel the pressure. We would always be aware of these moments because she would ask for one of her 'urgent biscuits' – a box of shortbread kept in Malcolm's bottom drawer. The biscuits might go untouched for several weeks at a time, but could just as easily be consumed in a day.

One would know when things were particularly bad because she would ring us both early in the morning and give the same list of tasks, meaning that by the time we reached the office, unless we spoke to each other first, Malcolm and I would be phoning the same numbers, often to find that Thelma had already made the call herself an hour earlier. Irritating though this could be, it was part of a system that left little room for error and meant we achieved in a day what twice the number of people might achieve in two. If this sounds arrogant, it was proved to be true. Thelma hated waiting for anything, everything had to have happened five minutes ago. She also expected the very highest levels of efficiency and competence, something that looked scary and untenable to those who didn't understand how we operated as a unit. 'How can you stand it?' was a question occasionally asked of both Malcolm and me. At the same time, what we lacked in financial gain was compensated for by the degree of power and freedom we were given, a situation that I think set us apart from our contemporaries.

We didn't have room to put our quotes on the wall, but we pulled Peter Daubeny's much-loved 'Nobody helps, nobody cares . . .' out of the filing box and stuck it up. During the mounting of that production it was often most apposite. Thelma never raised her voice, certainly never shouted. When she was angry, she would drop her voice an octave and deliver a sharp put-down; this we called 'going for the jugular'.

The days in that small room could be long. Thelma would avoid lunches out unless they were with potential investors or about publicity for the production. We had no money to spare and she also resented the time. Despite enjoying her vodka after work, she rarely drank during the day. Extended lunches filled her with irritation. When we were not happy in that room, a general sinking of spirits would occur as we began to climb up the stairs each morning. The cramped conditions did nothing to ease the Herculean tasks; not only were we working on *Three Sisters*, we were also planning the next production. I had learnt to emulate Thelma's wicked wit and infectious energy from the National Theatre days with varying degrees of success, and this helped drive one through difficult times.

Malcolm and I had code phrases. It was easy for us to spot what kind of day lay ahead as soon as she entered the room. 'Gospel,' he would say under his breath – this was shorthand for 'The gospel according to' which essentially meant that anything she said, however ridiculous, was to be unquestioningly agreed with. 'Tamayto, tomato' indicated particularly contrary moods. There were of course the unexpected entrances. 'Darlings, I feel sick!' It turned out that at breakfast, unable to find her glasses, she had poured herself a bowl of Go-Cat and added milk.

I missed the National because I missed the proximity to the plays and the sheer numbers of people we had worked with. Even at the Peter Hall Company we had inhabited a busier office space. Once a play had opened, Thelma and I would spend most evenings at the theatre, but during pre-production it could often feel like a very isolated process.

At the end of the day, we would invariably go for a drink. The Waldorf Hotel was just around the corner and we would head for 'the leather bar'. A waiter would approach with his round silver tray. 'Darling' (to her, everyone was darling), 'I'll have a double vodka, no tonic, no ice, and the child will have a glass of red wine.' When the drinks arrived and the waiter had gone, she would raise her glass and peer at it. 'Darling, what is that!?' 'It's a double vodka,' I would reply. 'Pea, if that's a double, I'm a Chinaman. Now go and get me a *proper* drink.' I would go to the bar and explain that although

*I* knew it was a double, and *he* knew it was a double, due to the size of the glass (large and wide) it looked to her like a single. He would then add another two shots. 'Now, darling, *that* is a double vodka.'

The more tired we were, the harder it was to leave the deep leather seats and head for home. 'One for the road, darling,' she would say on our third drink. We had no expenses, it was 'our' money, and drinking in the Waldorf wasn't cheap. Malcolm was in charge of the money – we called him 'Miss Moneypenny' – and he would often get beady with us if we did this more than once a fortnight. 'We won't tell him, darling,' she would say if we were on a roll, which meant she didn't give him the receipts.

Opening nights are nerve-racking. This one in particular, with so much riding on it for us. Though we knew by opening night that we had a fine production, the critics wouldn't necessarily agree. The more seats given away, the less money taken at the box office, and gifted seats were no guarantee of a partisan audience. We gave the minimum. The press were necessary, and decisions on where to seat particular critics would take considerable discussion. Often Thelma would move around in the stalls from seat to seat during a dress rehearsal and then, in the dark, whisper to Malcolm or me details of whom she wanted to sit where. Investors were prioritised, and seats were also given to members of the creative team and anyone who had done us a favour. We had little time to get ourselves ready between the final preparations and the arrival of the great and the good. I went to Thelma's and she found me something to wear from her collection of vintage dresses.

We were both in black 1930s dresses and wearing pearls. Thelma's were the real thing, mine the very good paste she had given me. We had tiny original period purses, large enough only for a lipstick and a little money. These clothes were part of a phase we went through and Thelma often picked out very fine frocks, blouses, jodhpurs and silk underwear for me at antique markets.

Thelma was probably at the height of her powers, famous in our world and with an aura of fame on the street. She would attract much attention and people with no idea who she was would certainly have the idea she was 'someone'. She could, however, turn it off as well as on, and was happy with what Malcolm and I referred to as her 'bag lady' persona. This look usually coincided with periods of considerable stress when she might end up wearing the same rather odd outfit for several days in a row and would have failed to find time to dye her roots. On one such occasion, as she was approaching the National stage door, Maggie Smith, mistaking her for a general factotum, threw Thelma her keys and asked her to park the car for her before disappearing inside.

We made our way nervously from backstage to the front-of-house. On entering the foyer we were spotted by one of our favourite older actors. Approaching, he opened his arms and embraced first Thelma, kissing her on both cheeks, and then me. I didn't have time to think about how to avoid my allocation of kisses, because there was not enough space between noticing the deposits that had been left on Thelma's cheeks before it was my turn. I had in an instant noticed the slightly brown secretions in each corner of his mouth, but hadn't thought what they might be until the realisation that whatever it was had now secured itself to Thelma's immaculately made-up face. The horror of then feeling it on mine prompted an almost immediate retch.

As we headed through the crowded foyer, I continued to retch, eyes watering. Bereft of a tissue, I would have to wait until we were seated to get one from Thelma, and I was already worrying about how to remove whatever it was in a discreet manner. I could see clearly the deposits on Thelma's cheeks – what if someone else came to kiss her – or me!

We kept moving, I was directly behind her, with my hands resting gently in the small of her back. Thelma would probably be oblivious; at least, that was my assumption. There was no hope of saying anything to her in the immediate aftermath because we couldn't hear each other above the din. And our lovely actor was probably still within earshot. I just had to hope that no one else would stop to say hello, and to my delight Thelma seemed, unusually, to be keeping herself to herself as we made good progress down the stairs to our seats in the stalls. By this time my mouth was filling with saliva, and whatever was on my cheeks had in my mind grown like a mushroom. I could feel this tighten its grip and my skin seemed to stretch as it dried. There was now no possibility of making it to the ladies before curtain-up.

We sat down at last, not having caught each other's eye or said a word to one another since leaving the foyer. I kept looking at her cheeks, and would then feel the retch swell again. Oh, for a wet wipe! I thought, and a moment of privacy to deal with the ever-tightening secretion. Unable to stand it any longer, I leant towards her. 'Thelma?' I whispered, and before I could complete the sentence she said very quickly and firmly, 'Shut up, shut up, shut up!' It was only in the interval that we were able to wipe our faces.

In those days nothing much beat the adrenalin rush that surged through my body as the curtain rose on our very own production, and this was the first in that category. It's a bittersweet experience, because much as there is the thrill of a new-minted performance, and despite having watched dress rehearsals, technical rehearsals and previews, the press night has a different energy – oddly, not always the best. There is also the nervousness around how it will be received, not just for ourselves, but for the actors and the creative team. We desperately wanted it to be a success for them too.

At the party afterwards it was necessary to stick closely by Thelma's side as she would sometimes fail to recognise people – she rarely wore her glasses on a first night. 'Our major investor is approaching you', 'The cultural attaché from the Russian Embassy is to your left', or 'You have just cut Ian McKellen dead'. The party wasn't a grand affair; we chose to have it in the theatre circle bar. Unfortunately, though Thelma tried her best, we were unable to use our own caterers (Thelma and me, filling a trolley in Marks & Spencer); theatre rules meant purchasing the wine and food directly from them.

The reviews were mostly excellent and, despite the Gulf War, which had threatened to empty theatres, we would end up with the 'House Full' signs outside the Queen's Theatre. The production made us a lot of money. Money we would lose on the next production.

Each evening before the performance, the company would gather in the Green Room. The lights would be turned off and a candle lit. These meetings were held in absolute silence. Thelma and I were allowed to join if we were at the theatre, and this was probably the only time, apart from her visits to church to light candles, when Thelma was ever silent. At the end they would all say, '*S bogum*' which means 'May God be with you' in Russian. This little ritual had been Robert's parting gift before he returned to Tbilisi.

The idea of abandoning the the actors after the press night was abhorrent to Thelma, so most evenings she was there and I usually accompanied her. There's a very particular atmosphere and energy backstage at a thea-tre prior to curtain-up. It's also quite a delicate place to be: one knocks on a dressing room door and enters the inner sanctum of an actor busily preparing themselves for a performance. Putting on make-up, having their wigs dressed, getting into costume. Very quickly you get to know those who are happy to chat and those who prefer to be left alone. Some actors will happily be talk-ing about anything right up until minutes before they are due on stage, others retreat into a very concentrated space, one you wouldn't dream of penetrating.

If Thelma couldn't be there, I would go alone. I was always nervous when it was just me, despite the fact I would get more used to doing the dressing room round as time went on and encountering and dealing with whatever problem might be waiting.

We arrived at the theatre one evening to find the wardrobe mistress, whose responsibility it was to put curlers in Vanessa's wig, in tears. Olga's wig was long ash blonde hair, sometimes plaited or piled on top of her head, and at certain points during the action she would let it down and brush it out. On this particular evening the wardrobe mistress had entered Vanessa's dressing room to discover her sitting there sporting a short crop. She had taken a pair of scissors and cut the hair off the wig, but although having decided that Olga would have had short hair, Vanessa still wanted the curlers put in, a task that was proving nigh impossible.

The wig cropping had been done without discussion with either Robert or Thelma, and having cost us £1,500 might not have been so easily tolerated had it not been a 'star's turn'. However, Olga now had short hair, and Vanessa was proved right: her performance as the kindly and maternal elder sister, a spinster who would have married anyone, even an old man, if only they had asked, was special and moved one to tears. It wasn't the short hair instead of the plaited hair that I noticed; but perhaps whatever Vanessa was searching for at that very moment within Olga's character was released for her the instant she cropped the wig, and maybe sometimes great performances emerge through simple actions like that.

Some evenings we would watch the entire play, but mostly we would watch either the first or the second half, and then repair to the bar. We would wait for our Company Manager Jeremy to come and give us the figures for the night; which were always good news on this production. I can still vividly recall moments from the play, most clearly the moving sight of the three sisters holding hands at the end.

Perhaps the wonderful thing about theatre is that it never can be repeated, and every performance differs from the one before. For me, this production released Chekhov from the museum, and I have yet to see a braver or more innovative version.

On the day of the final performance of the play in London, Thelma took a taxi to the old Covent Garden flower market at 4 a.m., just as she had done for the last night of every foreign production at the NT, to buy several large boxes of flowers. Once the curtain had gone up, we would divide the stems equally between two big plastic sacks, returning after the interval to a seat reserved for each of us in the boxes stage left and right, from where at the curtain call we could hurl the flowers onto the stage. This would come as a complete surprise to the actors, and they would stay behind long after the audience had left the auditorium, some tearful, picking them up in small bunches to take home.

With her usual brilliance, Thelma had secured Swiss funding for the production, contingent upon the company giving a number of performances in Zurich after the London run. Here we stayed in a rather splendid hotel and Thelma and I shared a room with a massive double bed. Another room would have cost considerably more, and Thelma saved wherever she could. This was rather a curate's egg, good and bad in parts. Good, because at this point in time I found everthing Thelma had to say fascinating, even if it was about her breakfast. But it meant I got little, if any, sleep. We were always late to bed as our Swiss hosts had arranged plenty of after-performance celebrations. By the time we did get to bed, Thelma would talk until at least 3 a.m., at which point she would promise a lie-in, usually meaning she would get up at 7 but refrain from talking to me until 7.30.

We would sometimes escape the theatre, and on one occasion she took me to the Fraumünster Church to see the five stained-glass windows by Marc Chagall. We dined in the Kronenhalle, which is full of Chagalls and Picassos. It was, according to Thelma, where Yeats took Maud Gonne. One day we walked higher up into an old part of the city and had the best fondue ever, accompanied by a very fine bottle of white wine. Thelma rarely drank wine, but if she did it had to be superb.

There's a strange grief that comes at the end of a production. When so many individuals are thrown together, an accelerated intimacy is formed, and for weeks the intensity of these relationships dominates one's life. With the ending one felt the impossibility of repeating the experience. But then, the theatre can be a fickle business.

# 20

## Fiona the Great

I was first introduced to Fiona Shaw in 1989 when Thelma and I had been to see her perform in Deborah Warner's production of *The Good Person of Szechwan* at the National. But our first proper meeting was in the stalls bar of the Queen's Theatre a year later during our production of *Three Sisters*. I had already seen Deborah's production of *King John* at the RSC, but not her much discussed and hugely successful production of *Electra*, with Fiona in the title role. Surely we should be working with these women. When they eventually came to meet us to talk about reviving *Electra*, I was excited but also a little nervous. They were a furnace of talent and, I had been told, rather formidable.

Thelma and I were amused when they asked for a glass of sherry each. Deborah brought me an umbrella with a map of the world printed on it and Thelma a pair of oven gloves. We'd met one night at the National when Deborah had asked Thelma about the marks on her hands and wrists, which turned out to be burns from her oven. The umbrella, meanwhile, was a symbol of our collective desire that *Electra* would be performed far and wide.

This production was very important for me as I was allowed to cut my teeth in more adventurous ways and given some small responsibility for budgets, and setting up the tour. To deal directly with Deborah about many

169

creative issues, as well as casting, was so important – I cared very much about it and worked incredibly hard. Never before had a director involved and included me in such detail about a set, or discussed strategies concerning all aspects of casting, and I had never worked with a director as charismatic as Deborah – a true artist who stops at nothing to achieve everything needed to make her vision come to life. Forensic about the detail, Deborah drove some colleagues to despair, but I relished the opportunity to be involved in such a unique process.

A short regional tour would be followed by a run at the Riverside Studios and finally we'd perform at the theatre in Bobigny, Paris. Due to the exacting nature of the design and Deborah's determination not to compromise her vision, we ended up performing in mostly unheated and previously unused spaces. A transport museum and a sports centre became temporary theatrical venues. In order to survive the evening, our audiences were handed blankets and advised to bring hot water bottles.

Money was tight and I was given the task of negotiating the designer's fee, though there was very little to actually negotiate as fees were set only a fraction above the Equity minimum. If enough people had said no, the project would have fallen apart. I gave my well-rehearsed preamble to the very tough agent. 'All right,' she said, interrupting me. 'How much?' When I gave her the figure there was a pause and then 'My God!' But she did say yes. This had nothing to do with my 'negotiating' skills and everything to do with Deborah's reputation as a director with whom people were very keen to work.

*

Fiona's hair was fashioned into tiny plaits very tight against her scalp, so tight in fact that she suffered headaches. She lost considerable weight and her costume, a beautifully simple black shift that exposed her arms and legs, along with the hair, gave her a particularly spectral appearance. Pomegranates and amaryllis were the only colour in Hildegard Bechtler's pale stone courtyard. There was withered grass between the stones and a single line of water, which ran through the centre of the stage in a narrow gully. From the moment Fiona pushed open the huge sliding door at the back of the set, heaving against it with all her might, to the moment she lay cradling the ashes of Orestes, her dead brother, there was no let-up to the disturbing levels of grief in this performance. But this Greek tragedy wasn't performed in any ritualistic manner, it was played as if it were all real life.

Fiona's performance as Electra proved to be the most upsetting and affecting single creation I had seen to date. Her visceral powers appealed to the heart and the mind with equal intensity. Her serious and natural intellect, matched by abundant wit and an extraordinarily rare take on the world, was the piston in her emotional engine. It was a new kind of acting for me, a rich, complex diet, not for the faint-hearted.

I was thrilled to join the company in Paris for the final part of the tour. This was to be my first trip out with a production and my expectations were dizzyingly high. During the curtain call on the opening night, Deborah joined the actors on stage and made a thank you speech to Thelma, who joined them to share the applause. I was witnessing for the first time Thelma's power and influence being matched – here were two women as brilliant as she was. This was also my first trip to Paris. I'd read Hemingway's *A Moveable Feast*, which inculcated a romantic notion of the city. I was poor and in Paris, working with artists who I believed were making history. The idea that I was being creative by proxy was intoxicating. This was the start of an enduring friendship with both Fiona and Deborah, which was to act as an ignition key to my growing independence.

Nobody made me laugh as much as Fiona did. The first time she invited me for supper, we ate pudding before the main course. She had woefully mistimed the cooking. The second time, unable to work out how to use her new oven, we sat staring at a pile of raw sausages and uncooked potatoes, before finally tucking into a bowl of salad and rummaging around for some cheese.

Fiona Shaw, the award-winning actress whose considerable talents onstage are matched by her intellectual abilities off – regularly asked to give lectures on the works of Shakespeare, the poetry of Yeats or Emily Dickinson, to join panels of intellectuals abroad to discuss art and literature – has a brain the size of Dublin. Yet the machinations of her everyday existence invariably prove challenging.

I rang her one morning. 'I can't talk now, Pea, I've been burgled – I'm onto the police!' her voice verging on the hysterical. She had returned to the flat from a meeting to find the doors from her study into the garden open. Various drawers in her filing cabinet were in disarray, and hundreds of euros required for a forthcoming trip were nowhere to be seen (I did point out later that keeping cash in a file marked 'EUROS' might have been foolhardy). The deeds to her house were also missing – she had left them on the table following a meeting with her solicitor earlier that morning. Fiona then noticed that the fencing at the end of her garden was broken and the compost pile trodden down.

She rang the police and reported the burglary. Moments later a neighbour appeared, to remind her that the fencing company had visited that morning to assess some planned works and to apologise for the mess. As she closed the door on her neighbour, the solicitor phoned to apologise for accidentally picking up the file with the deeds to her house as he had left, and said he would send them back to her. That only left the mystery of the missing euros. After a trawl through the filing cabinet, they were eventually found in the wrong hanging file. It happened that Fiona regularly left her garden doors unlocked and the wind had blown them open; the chaos was all of her own making.

The phone rang again; it was the police with a crime number, wanting more details of the burglary. Seized with panic and visions of fingerprint experts filling her flat and finding only one culprit – she blurted out, 'I'm cancelling that burglary!'

'Do you know how to get to Stansted Airport?' I asked Fiona the day before we were due to drive there to take a flight to Ireland. 'Yes, of course,' she replied in such a dismissive manner that I put the thought right out of my head.

The following morning, having driven for nearly an hour, with no idea whether we were even on the M25 and worried we were going to miss the flight ('Look at the signs going in the opposite direction!' Fiona screamed in desperation), I saw a pub marooned in the middle of a section of junctions. 'Let's ask in there,' I suggested – ignoring the fact it was only 8.30 a.m. 'Yes, but how do I get to it!' she said in desperate tones. By the time we'd negotiated the spaghetti loops of road, we found ourselves on an island surrounded by speeding cars. Leaping out of the car and making her way towards the pub entrance, she suddenly turned dramatically on her heel and raced back to the car, pursued by barking Alsatians.

# 21

## *Feast or Famine*

Until Alan Rickman visited our office and found three of us virtually sitting on top of one another, he had envisaged a rather large suite of offices, an illusion, he said, created by the phrase 'One moment, I'll put you through'. The first time he did visit our office, he found Thelma sitting on the old sofa in her bra, dictating to Malcolm while I made the tea.

Thelma had known Alan for some years, though not well. They got to know each other better when Thelma joined the Board of RADA, where Alan was Vice Chairman. At a meeting she and Alan were asked to have with a group of students, Alan introduced them both as follows:

'Hello, I'm Alan Rickman and I'm an actor. This is Thelma Holt, she's an actress who has been out of work for thirty years, but she's doing OK.'

As time went by, Alan, more than anyone I think we ever worked with, 'got' Thelma. He also made me laugh about her more than anyone else. 'WHAT ... is ... she ... talking about?' he would say in 'that voice' – Thelma had a habit of launching into a story, expecting the listener to have all previous knowledge of proceedings and know all the characters involved.

Alan was of course handsome, and sexy. But perhaps his most attractive quality, aside from his talent, was his genuine kindness, particularly to young actors and to actors who had not had his good fortune. He was always organising nights out to the theatre and suppers and invariably paid for everyone. Alan and his wife Rima were invited to all our company parties, even if he wasn't in the show. They supported our work and rarely missed an opening night. One of the first things I noticed about Alan was his hands, which were those of a young man. They didn't look as if they had ever held a tennis racket or a football, certainly never a power tool. But as he got older, his hands seemed to me to remain boy-like.

*Tango at the End of Winter* was a co-production with the Japanese. Director Yukio Ninagawa and his producer, Tadao Nakane, the team who had brought *Macbeth* and *Medea* to the National Theatre, were, for the first time, to work with English actors. Thelma Holt Ltd had made money with our very successful production of *Three Sisters*, and Thelma could now put her dream idea to the test.

This would be the only time we produced a new work. The play was by a Japanese writer called Kunio Shimizu, and the playwright Peter Barnes was engaged to adapt it for the London stage. When it came to casting the lead role, there was only one person Thelma ever wanted to play Sei, the washed-up middle-aged actor who, reluctant to face growing old, withdraws into a world of fantasy and memory. Alan Rickman was not a name that excited the Japanese; they'd never heard of him. She told them first about his hugely successful *Les Liaisons Dangereuses* with the RSC – she was met with blank faces and a lot of conferring. It wasn't going at all well, until she leant forward and said, '*Die Hard!*' She didn't have to say anything else.

Alan was becoming very big news, having just received fabulous reviews for his star turn as the Sheriff of Nottingham in Kevin Costner's film *Robin Hood: Prince of Thieves*. It was our bad luck that his fame had not quite reached its zenith. This, coupled with the fact that we were unable to secure a West End theatre with what we call 'passing trade', on either Shaftesbury Avenue or St Martin's Lane, meant that we ended up in what turned out to be the 'kiss of death', Piccadilly Theatre. Tucked away behind Piccadilly Circus, it also happened to be one of the largest theatres in London, with over a thousand seats on three levels.

The poster artwork for the production didn't help sell it either, being far too esoteric, in the form of a couple of shadowy figures in a tango embrace transposed on a peacock feather design. Neither did we make use of Alan's face, and unfortunately we agreed to alphabetical billing. The idea of the ensemble company is all very well in the subsidised sector and may work well with the right play in the right place and with the right number of stars in it. But having only one name with any real chance of attracting large audiences, lost down the cast list in the R position, proved in retrospect to be a foolhardy decision. Though the reviews were respectful, and some even very good, they were not enough to put the production on the theatrical map and we had to work very hard to get audiences in. We rarely played to more than four hundred.

Apart from Alan, we had a fine cast, including Robert Glenister, Barry Stanton, Suzanne Bertish and the wonderfully eccentric Peter Bayliss. Peter had a dog – he didn't actually – but he brought this imaginary creature to the theatre, so his dressing room had to be large enough to accommodate the dog, and the stage management had to make sure there was always a bowl filled with water. 'But what about the dog?' Thelma said while sorting dressing rooms in Edinburgh. It was written into his contract that the animal was allowed to accompany him on tour.

The Number One dressing room is nearly always given to the star of the production. Number One is predicated not upon its size or features, but simply its proximity to the stage. Some of these dressing rooms are almost small hotel suites, with two rooms and separate lavatories; others have merely enough space for a dressing table and a small divan. Alan Rickman's dressing room at the Piccadilly Theatre was not large, but it was the closest to the stage, therefore it was Number One.

The first time I visited him there I managed to knock over a pile of wine glasses he had neatly stacked atop a small trolley. Alan had been entertaining after a performance. He stood watching me as I picked them up and attempted to restack them. Just as I thought this task complete, and with Thelma chivvying me from the open door, I turned to him to say goodnight and upset the glasses again with several crashing to the floor. Bright red in the face, I apologised in some confusion. Alan continued to look at me and then in his treacle-dark laconic tones said simply, 'Have you quite finished?'

As always when money is in short supply, imagination and cunning are invaluable assets, and Thelma had both in almost equal measure. Wanting what she described as 'an environmental foyer', she hoped the audience would feel something of what they were about to experience as soon as they set foot in the theatre. The play was set in a disused cinema, which turned out to be apt because the Piccadilly in its early days operated as a cinema. Suzanne Bertish had friends at art school who produced wonderfully distressed old film posters mounted on thick cards and suspended from the roof. Thelma and I were at the theatre almost every night doing our rounds of the dressing rooms an hour before the show; Suzanne – in the habit of sitting without her top on – prompted Thelma to remark, 'That girl's got great tits, nearly as good as mine, darling.' However, when I did the rounds on my own, I found this eccentricity very embarrassing. Suzanne and her coterie were so at ease with their sexuality and seemed to be having the good time that was eluding me.

Thelma had found a little Italian restaurant not far from the theatre called the Piccadilly, no longer in existence. We would often eat there after the show, always ordering the same food as it was usually very late. We would devour a large plate of mozzarella, avocado and tomato and a bowl of chips between us. Occasionally members of the cast would join us, and sometimes the entire team would eat together.

Our recent move from the tiny room at the top of Catherine Street to the more glamorous accommodation of the Ivor Novello Suite in Waldorf Chambers, presided over by Duncan Weldon's organisation, gave us more room, a shared receptionist and kitchen. We occupied one room while a second, smaller office was filled with our box files, a fax machine, a desk and shelves full of plays and old copies of *Spotlight*.

We worked with typewriters for years, Thelma reluctantly agreeing to computers only after *Three Sisters* when Malcolm persuaded her by stressing how much time we could save. But she never trusted them. 'Can I have the contract for X?' she would ask. She liked things on paper; she liked to see us go to a filing cabinet, pull out a cardboard hanging file and provide her with the necessary paperwork. 'Is it in there?' she would say, pointing accusingly at the computer. She hated waiting for it to print out – 'Pea, why is it in there?' she would ask while Malcolm went to the printer to retrieve the requested document. She would then look at it as though it were some kind of copy: 'Where's the original? I want to make sure nothing's changed.' By which time Malcolm was in pieces.

Likewise with email – she didn't understand that at all. She was a great letter writer, trusting that Malcolm was able to convey her tone of voice in a typed letter, something that would somehow get lost the moment it vanished, unsigned, into his computer. If Malcolm suggested an email so that the recipient got it immediately, a look of total disbelief would cross her face. 'But where has it gone? – Is it in there? – How will so and so get it?'

The office microwave was another source of concern to her. She preferred a plate of cold food. But if Malcolm heated a microwavable meal, she wouldn't want to eat it – particularly if it was meat. She considered heating flesh quickly from the inside out utterly wrong.

When Thelma needed a more impressive room for an important meeting, she would borrow either Duncan's or the rarely used bedroom containing nothing but a double bed, a phone and a large mirror. The first time Thelma had a meeting with the Japanese in there, they all got down on all fours and looked under the bed. She loved conducting interviews in that room, often interrupting them midway by summoning me to ask questions such as, 'Darling, I'm not difficult, am I?' or 'Darling, am I a feminist?' Most memorably, while sprawled luxuriously on the bed, she asked me with wide-eyed mischief, 'Darling, she wants to know how I relax?' and before I could answer she suddenly exclaimed, 'Well, darling, I like to lie on my bed and stroke my pussy!' – I speedily added the word 'cat' to the stunned-looking journalist. Thelma seemed oblivious to the double entendre.

Duncan Weldon's West End productions and tours were always star-led, often with major American names – Lauren Bacall, Jack Lemmon, Al Pacino, to name but a few. Having already worked together with Peter Hall and Richard Harris, Duncan and Thelma had a mutually respectful relationship, but they couldn't have been more different. Duncan was shy, and although very comfortable around theatre people, could appear socially awkward outside those circles. He would pull on his beard, his left hand tucked under his chin, and say 'What, what' before delivering an incredibly wry statement. His deputy, Peter Wilkins, was blisteringly efficient, and his two assistants, Sheila and Gina, were consistently capable and tolerant.

Sheila was on the phone to Lauren Bacall one morning as I hovered with a question – 'Yes, Betty, I have got you a pair of house seats for the performance tomorrow night', then 'No, he's not free, Betty', to which Bacall growled, 'Well, who the hell am I gonna go with?' By now I understood that fame and fortune did not equal an absence of loneliness, but if you had asked me to imagine such a conversation fifteen years earlier when I stood by the Stilton in Harrods watching Lauren Bacall the movie star buy cheese, I would not have been able to comprehend it.

Major stars were often found wandering around the corridors in Duncan's offices. Thelma and I were playing catch with an old tennis ball one afternoon; I had my back to the open door and heard a voice I recognised asking where Duncan could be found. As a family we'd watched *Some Like It Hot* and *The Apartment* so many times we could quote whole chunks of dialogue: 'You tore off one of my chests!', 'I'm a boy, I'm a boy, oh God I'm a boy!' 'That's the way it crumbles, cookie-wise.' When I turned around, there he was in tan chinos and a matching Harrington jacket, an old man, but still Jack Lemmon.

Vicki, our young receptionist, whom Malcolm and I nicknamed Bubble, stuttered and stammered inaudibly the more nervous she became, but managed to take most of our teasing with good grace. The building had an old gated lift, a relic of Ivor's day; it was so small it seemed certain one would die of asphyxia. One morning, this lift being out of order, Malcolm had climbed the many stairs carrying a huge pile of mail under his arm. As he passed Vicki's desk, she asked, 'What's that?' 'It's half a pound of liver sausage,' Malcolm replied without hesitation.

As a production, *Tango* was as avant-garde as Thelma herself and there were episodes in that play as vivid in my memory as at the time. There was a scene where Alan danced the tango with a beautiful young Beatie Edney, both dressed in black and white, and lit by a blue-white light against the rows of empty cinema seats designed as part of the set; it was hauntingly beautiful. Equally stunning were the carefully choreographed slow-motion sequences where young actors would move and fall in the derelict cinema to the strains of Pachelbel's Canon in D. This was true theatrical magic, and whatever financial worries were going on backstage, watching these scenes induced in me feelings both romantic and unreal. I would watch them over and over again; this really was my drug of choice.

All such visions came at a cost. With a cast of over twenty, the costume budget was considerable. Even so, some of the actors found the simplicity of the clothes unappealing. Thelma came up with a stroke of genius that saved money and resulted in the clothes flying off the costume designer's rails. Thelma's idea was to cut the labels out of less exciting items and replace them with designer labels. So a bunch of scarves the design team had picked up at the Tie Rack at Heathrow Airport were transformed into Kenzo and Chanel. Simple black jackets and coats became Comme des Garçons and Issey Miyake. Soon it was impossible to discern the originals from the fakes and by the end of the run actors were begging to keep their costumes.

The lighting design was costly; bringing an entirely Japanese creative team to London was hugely expensive, while employing not one but two writers was off the Richter scale, causing Thelma to comment, 'I prefer working with dead writers, darling.' Furthermore, it had become clear early on in rehearsal that we would have to employ a choreographer both for the all-important tango scene and for all the dreamlike set pieces.

Thelma used her inimitable powers of seduction and guile to secure financial backing both here and in

Japan – where three-quarters of the half a million it cost to mount was raised. Once during the raising of the money she was in a restaurant with Valerie Grove, who was doing an interview with her for the *Sunday Times*. We had taken a call at the office from some Japanese financiers with whom she was meant to be meeting, wondering where she was. Malcolm called the restaurant.

'Anyone here called Thelma Holt?' the waiter had asked the room at large.

Thelma was very good at widening her eyes and looking innocent. 'She left ten minutes ago by taxi,' she said, before confiding in Valerie Grove that in order to get on in the theatre business there were times when one had to be economical with the truth. 'Oh yes, darling, honesty is the worst policy.'

Alan became a major factor in fundraising and was good at attending promotional events when Thelma felt it necessary to 'wheel him out', as she called it. At a small dinner hosted by Nakane at a very smart Chinese restaurant, Alan's presence was once more required. Not many were there: two very important people from the Japan Foundation with an interpreter, Ninagawa, Peter Barnes and his partner, Alan, Thelma and myself. Nakane, considering himself a bon viveur, had taken charge of ordering while we sat eating, as course after course arrived. I was between Thelma and Alan watching a large platter being brought towards our table. This dish, Nakane had told us all, was a particular delicacy. As three waiters made space in the centre of the table, the fourth hovered with the platter of what looked alarmingly like a pile of tiny bird heads, complete with beaks and crinkly burnt eyes. It couldn't be! But as the dish was placed carefully in the centre of the table, my worst fear was confirmed. Thelma said, 'Oh my God!' at which point I dived under the table between Alan and Thelma's legs. She speedily covered the dish with a large white napkin. Amid a lot of confusion and sharp intakes of breath, Thelma explained that I had a serious bird phobia. 'We call her Tippi Hedren, darlings.' There would be no possibility of my sucking the brains out of small fried birds' heads. Once the dish had been removed, Alan put his head under the table: 'It's all right, you can come out now.'

Because of the scale of Ninagawa's work and the set he planned for the production, our rehearsals took place at Three Mills Studios, a venue large enough but a considerable distance for everyone to travel to. At the same time, an independent television company was filming a documentary about our production. Thelma allowed them very limited access to rehearsals, protective of her actors and of Ninagawa's privacy and methods of working. The documentary crew followed us to the Edinburgh Festival, where we were to play prior to the West End. Hopes were high; a mixed blessing, as expectation can create disappointment.

In Edinburgh, Thelma and I stayed in a room at the very top of an adequate B&B. 'Darling, I hope there isn't a fire or we're fucked,' she said one night as we reached our garret after yet another climb up the many stairs. After a very long day and a late night with the company, she promised we would not have to be up early the following morning. It was a Saturday and there was a market she wanted to visit. 'Darling, it doesn't open until ten, so we can have a leisurely breakfast and then set off.' At two thirty in the morning the lights went out. The last thing I heard as I drifted off was Thelma telling me that the Japanese found the way we smelt off-putting. 'It's the milk, darling, it makes us smell funny to them, they don't like it.'

What seemed like moments later I woke to a very strong smell, difficult to identify at first. The room seemed unnaturally quiet and I wondered if it was still the middle of the night. As my eyes focused, a light appeared and a sulphurous smell seemed to be very close by. Thelma was speaking to me, and as I turned over she was there, holding a plate with a hard-boiled egg on it, right under my nose. 'Darling, I got you an egg before the rush.' Still not fully awake, I asked her the time. 'It's a quarter to seven, darling.' I thought, ruefully, that my idea of a later start was not quite the same as Thelma's.

Thelma fought to keep *Tango* on, even when it was haemorrhaging money. Despite the lack of 'bums on seats', this production was one of our happiest and I still cannot listen to Pachelbel's Canon in D without being transported back to the Piccadilly Theatre, and most of all to the dance that cost us so much.

On our return to London from Edinburgh, I finally got a later start. In fact, when we'd had a run of particularly late nights at the theatre, as was often the case with *Tango*, I would get to go in an hour or so later. This was a luxury. As there were four of us at the flat, bath times had to be negotiated, though generally I had first call in the morning with Fifi bathing at night; Hodie always left before anyone else was up. Charlie was a student and late riser. My day would begin with a hot bath and a cup of tea – I also had the flat to myself.

The bathroom at Westbourne Terrace was very large with a window looking out over the rooftops and balconies at the back of Gloucester Terrace. The bath itself was huge, 1930s pea green with a large elaborate mixer tap. There were frequent plumbing problems at Westbourne Terrace, resulting in calls to Mr Heap. Whatever the time of day he would head straight for the bathroom and evacuate his bowels.

On this particular morning as I lay back and added more water, there was a strange gurgling sound – not unusual – but then the flow became a trickle. I sat up and turned the tap off and then immediately on again, and lay back. It ran normally, then all of a sudden lumps started dropping out of the tap with accompanying feathers. I scrambled out of the bath screaming as bits of dead pigeon bobbed about in the water. I rang Mr Heap who said he couldn't come until the following morning, but not to use the water. I left notes everywhere and went to work. Thelma ignored my problem, but told me the reason she never ate mackerel was because they fed on dead sailors. The following morning Mr Heap found another dead pigeon in the tank. I brushed my teeth with bottled water for weeks afterwards.

# 22

## *Alan Rickman Loses His*
## Die Hard *Jacket*

Thelma is an anagram of Hamlet. This is acci-
dental, but her passion for Shakespeare was
not, *Hamlet* and *Macbeth* being two of her favourite
plays. At the start of her career she had performed
in both at the Open Space Theatre and was always
quoting from them: 'Listen, darling, I know a hawk
from a handsaw' was said at least once a week
when she considered someone was trying to 'screw'
her.

When Alan Rickman played Hamlet with Robert
Sturua directing, it was a happy production and sold
out long before we opened at the Riverside Studios.
It wasn't an enormous critical success, and perhaps
Alan suffered more than he might have done had
the director been English. His relationship with
Thelma became very close and enduring. I have a
theory that this was partly based upon his ability
to tell her exactly what he thought, even if it meant
sometimes being a little critical. His honesty and open-
ness left no room for ambiguity, and she respected
that.

After a dress rehearsal of *Hamlet*, we headed for the
bar at the Riverside and gradually the cast emerged.
Thelma and I stood at the bar discussing what we
had seen. Alan, Geraldine McEwan and various other

members were settled round a table having a drink. As we talked I was very aware of Alan's continuing gaze but we stayed rooted to the spot and didn't join them. Later, clearly irked, he told us that we should have come and spoken to them, not kept our thoughts to ourselves. He was right and I learnt a lesson. Alan told me that Thelma always insisted later that we paid him £350 per week, but in fact we had only paid him £250 – 'Just make that perfectly clear would you,' he said with a hint of irony.

The budget was tight, so tight in fact, that Thelma decided we could cut costs by having me design the poster. This was further encouraged by the fact that Alan had studied Graphic Design at the Royal College of Art. 'Darling,' she said to him one morning on the phone, 'Pea's doing something with your face from *GQ* magazine and blowing it up on the photocopier.' Alan had recently done a fashion photo shoot for them and so with their permission we used one of their photographs. Thelma, Alan and I sat up very late one night in a Polish restaurant on the Goldhawk Road, turning bits of paper over and messing about with typefaces. Such was the extent of the print design meeting. Then our friend Michael Mayhew, king of graphics at the National Theatre, turned it into a poster. Despite its simplicity, it is one of those she became most proud of. 'The Pea did that, cost us fuck all,' she would say to anyone admiring it on our office wall.

Thelma's 'company' parties were notable for their abundance of alcohol and lack of food. She always insisted, as we rushed a trolley round the aisles of Marks & Spencer's food hall, that one carrier bag would feed five people. I questioned this when the carrier bag concerned contained only mini scotch eggs and cherry tomatoes.

Food was never a priority for Thelma because it got in the way of more important matters, like talking. She also takes a very poor view of spending her investors' money on fancy parties, so it was usually a case of let them eat scotch eggs and drink cheap wine (or as she referred to it, diesel fuel).

Having said that, these get-togethers were without exception great fun and everyone left happy, bonded – albeit temporarily – and inebriated. Jeremy and I would usually start washing up if nobody showed any sign of leaving by 2 a.m. The downside of these events (Malcolm, sensibly, rarely got involved) was that we had to turn up bright and breezy in the office the following morning, unlike the cast, who would often still have a hangover when they arrived for the following evening's performance.

On one of these occasions, the *Hamlet* party, Thelma, already in her nightdress and without shoes, was saying goodnight to Alan, who was the last to leave. Jeremy was particularly keen to get home as he was due to celebrate an anniversary with his partner, and to that end had a dozen roses and a bottle of champagne in his car. Thelma, followed through the door to her flat by a relieved Jeremy – the end was in sight – and her beloved cats Poppy and Psyche, was kissing Alan good-night when the door closed with a bang behind them. It was 3 a.m. and she was locked out in a state of undress with two cats and Jeremy – whose car keys were also inside and who was therefore unable to go home with the roses and champagne.

Alan, being the gentleman he was, took off his *Die Hard* crew jacket, draped this around her shoulders and suggested that they go to his house, which was just round the corner, where they could both spend the night. Thelma was having none of this, and upon arrival at Alan's was insistent on coming to me for the night – I was also just around the corner (a mixed blessing). Unfortunately, I had turned my phone and answer machine right down so that I wouldn't get disturbed too early the following morning (which was, unusually, a Sunday). This was not just on my account – my flatmates were all incredibly patient about my unsociable hours.

My efforts were in vain. At 7 a.m. the following morning the intercom went long and loud. Thelma was on the end of it and simply said, 'Ring me at the Hilton', before promptly disappearing again. I had no idea what she was talking about – until I played the answer machine and found twelve messages, all from an increasingly desperate Alan Rickman – the last one saying simply, 'Sweetpea, pick … up … the … fucking … phone.' There were two further messages from Thelma at the Hilton, and she wasn't happy.

I try to picture the look on the faces of the reservation staff in the early hours of that Sunday morning when Thelma appeared barefoot in a nightdress and a *Die Hard* jacket, with Jeremy holding the two cats. They spent the night in a double bed (a double room was all that was available on that busy Saturday night), Jeremy in his underpants, with the cats in drawers on a towel. Thelma was furious with me for not having received her messages. Her cleaner had the only spare key, so I had to pull a coat on over my pyjamas and get a taxi to the office in order to get her telephone number from the

Rolodex (Thelma was also furious with Malcolm for not having this number in his head; Malcolm could store a lot of numbers in his head).

Alan told me later that it took months to get his *Die Hard* jacket back.

# 23

## *Does She Look Like Julie Christie?*

The boyfriend had been a disguise for some time for my gayness and I was struggling with coming out. There were few women in the business who were 'out', so role models were hard to find. Certainly gay men and women were more visible working backstage than they were in front of the curtain, but even so, actors – particularly women – were more hidden. I felt the need to announce the fact to my parents, so planned a trip home. It was summer so I took a few days off and bought a very nice bottle of white wine. Having told them there was something important to discuss, their excitement induced further stress since my fear was that they thought I was going to announce my engagement to Tom, of whom they had grown rather fond. I poured us each a glass of wine and we sat in their garden in the hot sun. It's all a blur except for the bit when Mum said, 'Darling, if you love a donkey I don't mind if it makes you happy.' My father, clearly not wishing to be outdone, and then on his third glass of chilled wine, boomed, 'We don't mind if you are shagging sheep as long as you are happy!'

This was the summer of 1992 and we had just finished presenting Ariane Mnouchkine's *Les Atrides* at an old mill outside Bradford. It had been a real event and made more so by the heatwave we were caught in. It was so hot that we had to hand out bottles of water because people were passing out during the performances. On the opening night David Mellor fell asleep on Thelma during the performance and his shirt stuck to his body. 'Not a pretty sight, darlings,' Thelma would note.

I remember vividly the atmosphere of this victorious challenge, and it was the best of times. Thelma was relaxed, although probably a little bored as she preferred to get her teeth into a big problem to pass the time, and there really weren't any big problems for her to solve on this occasion. There was a field full of cows next to the mill and Thelma had a meeting with Ariane on a blanket. One of the technicians came back into the building after lunch and said to me, 'There are two more cows in the field and they're lying on a tartan rug.'

Back in London a few weeks later and busy working on our next production, Thelma and I were having a late-night curry in Westbourne Grove. I had slept with a woman for the first time. These were the days when Thelma and I spoke freely and I told her everything. So it was not unusual for me to share confidences like this, and the only reason for my slight apprehension was because of my own unresolved feelings about it all. The conversation went as follows:

SP: Thelma . . . I've met a woman . . .

TH: Really, darling . . . What kind of woman?

SP: A woman I am attracted to. I mean, I think I have fallen in love with a woman . . .

TH: Oh my God! [*head in hands*] I knew you were bored, I'll have to find you more work to do.

SP: No, Thelma, I'm serious, I mean I've been to bed with her.

TH: Darling . . . you're not gay. I'm telling you, Pea, you
are not gay. It's just a phase, darling. I mean, we've all
been there, but it's a cul-de-sac, darling, I'm telling
you it's a cul-de-sac. Oh my God . . . Is she attractive?
SP: Of course she is, she's really good-looking . . .
TH: Darling [*emphatic tone*], I mean [*pause, as if talking to an idiot*] does she look like Julie Christie? I
mean, what's the point otherwise?

By this time Tom and I had talked things through
and made our peace. He wasted no time getting himself a proper girlfriend and we remained close friends.
I think it was a relief for him to find that I was gay, as
this somehow made sense for him as to why I had never
been able to commit to him.

Quite why I later decided to find myself attracted to a
woman called Elsa who was ten years my senior and
had a fast, high-end lifestyle, is something that I knew
perplexed my family and friends. This may have been
like a panic-buy on my part, as I had been attracted to
many women but has often paralysed to do anything
about it.

When I became brave enough to make a move, for a
time I fixed on someone totally unsuitable for me and
out of my frame of reference. Elsa was such a person.
We were both, for very different reasons, lost souls.
She had for some time been unsettled and considering
a return to her native Sweden, and I – still something
of a closet queer, and lacking much experience – completed what was a hopeless match. The inequalities and
differences in our personalities, interests and thinking
hindered rather than helped my coming-out process. I

was uncomfortable and unliberated. Having spent most weekends drinking cider in a pub on the Portobello Road with Tom, Charlie, Hodie and Oliver and cooking feasts at Westbourne Terrace with Fifi, I found myself hanging out in the Oyster Bar at Bibendum, sipping champagne and wondering why Elsa kept disappearing to the loo.

As a private chiropractor, Elsa's client list was peppered with luminaries from all walks of life. On one occasion she was called to work on the set of a film with a remit to keep the stars in top condition. The leading actress turned out to be someone she had a crush on. This, coupled with her over-indulgence the previous night, led to her vomiting on the actress's back mid-massage. I believe Elsa's compulsion to relay this 'drama' resulted from the discovery that I had worked with and was now a close friend of the victim.

But I'm sure she too might have been surprised to find that the tall slender and sophisticated-looking young woman she'd allowed herself to become involved with was not sophisticated at all – and a tenderfoot and a hypochondriac to boot.

I used to hold my breath and count. Thinking that something terrible might happen unless I could hold my breath long enough to reach the next bus stop – or perhaps the sign a few yards further on; often extending the mental challenge until I was gasping for breath. Sometimes a thought would enter my head and I would have to touch a piece of wood in the superstitious belief that the horror could then be averted. This was tricky on the Tube or upstairs on the number 23 bus home. So I would hold my head, fingertips to each temple, three seconds on each side, and count while saying to myself: 'Touch wood, everything *will* be all right, touch wood everything *is* going to be all right.' I would also repeat this ritual every night before switching the light out.

My bed – apparently inspired in equal parts by *Mad Max* and *Alice in Wonderland* – was a present from Hodie, who at the time was engaged in building a huge gothic film set. Each corner consisted of large torched and polished wooden posts, topped with a combination of candelabras made from twisted chains and a copper lavatory cistern float. At one end a mirror, at the other once-molten metal embossed into a wooden plaque, declared: SWEETPEA'S BED.

It's a wonder I ever pulled, a further wonder they risked the bed. The first time Elsa did, I woke up with terrible chest pains and an ache down my left arm. I had read about this somewhere, it's what happens when you are having a heart attack. I woke her up; 'I think I'm having a heart attack.' She rang the doctor and explained the symptoms. We waited for about an hour and at 1.30 a.m. a doctor climbed the fifty-seven stairs to the top flat to find a slender and perfectly healthy-looking twenty-six-year-old propped up in a bed the likes of which I suspect he'd never seen. Fifi was also awake and hovering.

The doctor listened to my chest, took my blood pressure and checked my pulse. He put his stethoscope away carefully and said:

'How old are you?'

'Twenty-six,' I replied.

'Do you smoke?'

'No.'

'Do you take exercise?'

'Yes.'

'Why do you think you are having a heart attack?'

'Because I had a pain down my left arm and my chest is tight.'

'And why do you think this means you are having a heart attack?'

'I read it somewhere.'

He took two paracetamol out of his bag and asked Fifi to fetch a glass of water. He fixed me with a firm but not unfriendly gaze as I swallowed the tablets. He was more bewildered than irritated. 'There is nothing wrong with you,' he said as he left. The next day, Hodie said, 'There *is* something wrong with you – your head needs examining!'

# 24

## *Much Ado About Nothing*

There was something revolutionary about the way Thelma worked, although with her determination to produce only Shakespeare and the classics in the commercial sector she appeared a kind of theatrical dinosaur. She lived and worked by some strange religion all of her own, made up of Shakespearean quotes, the lighting of candles under St Anthony of Padua and her all-important 'built-in shit-detector'. She trusted few and relied on nobody.

Perhaps all truly pioneering spirits, particularly women, are alone. For the twenty years we worked together, when Malcolm and I were her left and right hand, although I knew we were vital I also believed that Thelma always felt, and ultimately was, without equal and alone. Our past hits and misses live on in the museum of my mind, along with the image of her on a number 23 hop-on hop-off bus from Westbourne Grove – her thinking time away from the telephone – pen in hand, jotting down the budget for our next production on the back of an envelope.

She rarely omitted to say 'Morning, darlings' as she swept into the office. Advance warning of potential trouble would be the sound of her approach heralded by her humming the 'Ode to Joy' from Beethoven's Ninth Symphony. She said that if this piece of music suddenly came into her head, something was going to go wrong.

On those occasions one of us would immediately go and make her a milky cup of coffee and serve it with an urgent biscuit. The need for a biscuit wasn't always a bad sign; sometimes it might just be the excitement of Thelma's creative plotting. Thelma didn't worry, she might have a background feeling that something wasn't right, but she would always do something about it. She was never interested in apportioning blame or looking backwards. 'I don't want a post mortem!' she would begin any conversation relating to a cock-up.

Her decision to produce *Much Ado About Nothing* was made more exciting by the fact that this would be the first time Shakespeare's play had been performed on Shaftesbury Avenue for forty-eight years.

A young up-and-coming director called Matthew Warchus would direct. Thelma had seen his work at the West Yorkshire Playhouse and was impressed. Matthew would arrive for meetings in our office like a brand-new bar of soap – pristine jeans and immaculately ironed shirts with an impressive crease down each arm. He was very particular, and knew exactly what he wanted. He didn't seem to warm towards Thelma or to particularly *get* her. No matter, perhaps, because the play was the thing and he did that very well indeed.

We had a terrific cast, headed by Janet McTeer and Mark Rylance (who went on to win Best Actor at the Olivier Awards that year), an unlikely and comical pairing for Beatrice and Benedick. Paul Taylor in a review for the *Independent* noted: 'The play's sparring duo here constitute a sort of Little and Large Show, for Rylance's gauche, hack-haired, bandy-legged bantam of a Benedick is a good head shorter than Janet McTeer's splendidly off-hand, Junoesque Beatrice . . .'

Janet and I became friends during this production. We would meet on Sunday evenings at her place or mine and eat roast chicken and share stories, usually about our then similarly shambolic love lives. It was Janet who persuaded me that spider plants announced student accommodation so I jettisoned them all immediately.

According to her, I had the coolest flat in London (once the spider plants had gone), but I wore the oddest clothes and always looked cross. Later, when I left Westbourne Terrace, I lived on the ground floor of her house with the new girlfriend Janet had introduced me to at one of our suppers. 'I've asked another couple of friends over this evening,' she announced as we anointed yet another chicken. They were late so I asked where they were coming from. 'Stoke Newington,' she replied, draining the broccoli. 'Are they gay?' I said. 'Yes! But how did you know?' 'Malcolm told me that lots of lesbians live in Stoke Newington.' I was still uneasy around my own sexuality and frankly didn't meet enough gay women, at least not knowingly. There was something rather magnificent about Janet; at just over six feet tall and incredibly striking, she also had that very particular charisma, even before she became a star.

*Much Ado* was a fine production, but not an overly happy one. There were tensions – although to be perfectly honest, I cannot remember why. Egos in the theatre can be top-heavy and there are clashes – even huge battles of will. 'You are too nice for this business,' Thelma had said to me in jest over lunch one day at the National. 'If you want to be liked, then get out of the theatre.' I had worried for days afterwards about her nailing a deep flaw in me that was going to prevent me from developing. This was one of her great skills, to be so loved and at the same time to be able to go for the jugular and not care what people thought of her. Caring about what people thought did not get plays on stage.

Neither Janet nor Mark was famous then, and neither was David Morrissey, who played Claudio, but they were well known and respected actors. However, there wasn't a name in the production that would guarantee enough 'bums on seats' to secure us financial success.

Thelma never threw money at things; we never had the money to throw. She and Janet went to Top Shop and bought dresses. Matthew had set the play roughly in the thirties, Janet knew what suited her and was not going to leave it entirely to the costume designer. The front-of-house display, a not insignificant budgetary consideration for any production, was a huge canvas version of the blinded Cupid, painted and erected by my brother and his then partner, a scenic artist. It certainly stood out among the shiny boards and displays on the Avenue at that time. They got reimbursed for the materials and a credit in the programme, but gave their time willingly. Hodie still has a lamp Thelma gave him from the set.

This is the kind of work I hope Thelma will be remembered best for. As Paul Taylor said at the end of his review: 'The blinded Cupid which runs as a motif through the beautiful sets has had its sight restored by the end; this commercial production, too, will be an eye-opener for anyone who believes that top quality Shakespeare is synonymous with the subsidised sector.'

After the production had closed, Janet came to our offices with thank you gifts for us. Mine was a ring accompanied by a card, written in her flamboyant hand, which I promptly read:

> *Dearest Pea,*
> *Thank you, you stunning bitch*
>   *Love*
>   *McTeer*

'Ah,' I said, looking at her, 'that's a lovely thing to say.' She looked confused.

'What!' she said.

'Stunning,' I replied. She roared with laughter.

'*Stringy* bitch!' she screamed.

When Hodie had moved out of the flat to live with his first serious girlfriend, he'd kept his room on, as a safety net. Amusingly, he was already earning far more money than me, though admittedly that wasn't hard to do. So for a while we had the luxury of an empty room.

When eventually he felt safe enough to let the room go, I rented it out to an actress. This was something I always swore I wouldn't do – I didn't want to live with any actors. But there was something about Bronagh Gallagher. She had just returned from LA where she had a small part in the film *Pulp Fiction*. When they met, Quentin Tarantino had no actual role available for her. However, he was so taken by her chutzpah that he elevated a small part for her so he could have her in the film. When we auditioned her for a role in a forthcoming production of *Peer Gynt* she walked into the theatre in a black suit with a white shirt and a pair of spats, with black bangs and red lipstick. She didn't know London, and when she got the role, booked herself into a hotel just around the corner from me in Westbourne Terrace.

On the first day of rehearsal she arrived with no make-up, hair tucked into a beanie hat, wearing a fifties American leather jacket and a pair of steel-toe-capped shoes. Full of stories, she was a complex mix of wild innocence and wisdom beyond her years. I marched up to her and said if she wanted to save herself a lot of money there was a room for rent in my flat for a fraction of what she was paying at the hotel. She said she would think about it. Two weeks later I invited her to come and see the flat. She arrived as I was taking a chicken out of the oven and opening a bottle of red wine. We talked for hours and she moved in the following week.

At a company party at Thelma's, Bronagh and I drank vodka – I had never drunk vodka. These were small shots of different-flavoured vodkas someone had given Thelma: pepper, lemon, raspberry. The following morning it took me twice as long to get to work because I had to keep getting off the Tube as the nausea took hold. Thelma took me out for breakfast and insisted I drank something disgusting called Underberg (a digestif bitter), which she maintained was the best cure for a hangover. I drank the small bottle in one as directed, and then went to the loo and was terribly sick. Bronagh, meanwhile, had an audition, and when we reconvened later that evening she confided that the hat I complimented her on was there only to hide the remnants of vomit in her hair that she had not had time to wash out.

# 25

## *The Birds*

After Hodie moved out, Charlie continued the late-night drug-fuelled gatherings, but I could no longer tolerate them. Eventually I asked him to move out, which was a terrible shock to him and he didn't speak to me for a while. But a few months later he thanked me for 'putting a rocket up my arse'. He found a nice basement flat just around the corner and sometimes on a fine night with the windows open, we could hear the sound of his parties, floating up the terrace.

We now had another empty room. Jeremy – who had been promoted to General *and* Company Manager – had a personal crisis when his partner left him and needed breathing space to sort things out. I was very fond of Jeremy, and I knew he would be the perfect flatmate. He didn't say yes straight away, but a week or so later asked me one night in the theatre if I had been serious. He moved in and took two rooms, which he made very comfortable and chic. I loved everything about having him there, except his 'Take That' phase.

By then, Fifi was the only person in the flat who wasn't working for Thelma Holt Ltd. Jeremy was now also the only man, but he wasn't that practical so I needed to remember to do things that I had previously relied on Hodie for. Like bleeding the many old radiators that gurgled and banged when the heating first came on (or not) like clockwork on 1 October. I had purchased a radiator key for the purpose.

I started in the main living room and began to slowly turn the small screw until I heard the hissing sound I'd been told about, and before long some black liquid seeped out into the cup I was holding carefully in position. I loosened the screw a little more and then it shot out and before I had time to understand exactly what had happened a powerful jet of water was spurting out of the radiator. I screamed for Fifi, who started grabbing tea towels, the washing-up bowl, anything to catch the unrelenting gush of water. Soon it was running through the floorboards into the flat below.

We were hysterical at this point. I was holding towels against it with all my strength, but this didn't stop the flow. Fifi took over and I called Hodie. 'Jesus Christ, you fucking idiot!' He was working and couldn't come over. I called Mr Heap who was at the pub. He'd had eighteen pints. He said if we paid for the minicab he'd come over immediately. When he arrived he found the screw in the bottom of the mug of black liquid and put it straight back into the radiator.

One morning I was not expected at the usual time as I'd worked late at the theatre the previous night. I had heard Jeremy making quite a bit of noise outside my room. I didn't get up, but I was aware that whatever he was doing was rather physical and that he was trying to be quiet. I dozed off again and by the time my alarm went off, the flat was silent, everyone had gone to work. I got up and made a cup of tea before going upstairs to run a bath. As I reached the large landing at the top of the stairs, I had the distinct impression that I was being watched. I looked around, and then I saw them.

To my right and above me on top of the tall cupboards on the landing were two pigeons. Someone had left the bathroom window open. Clearly, Jeremy had been corralling them up the stairs in an attempt to get them to leave via the open window. I panicked, dropped the tea and ran back downstairs. I felt sick and started sweating. I heard wings flapping and then silence. Cautiously I went back upstairs; they were gone from the cupboard. But one, with wings outstretched, was hurling itself against the glass of the bathroom window and failing to find the open half. I ran downstairs and let myself out of the flat. I stood outside, wondering what to do. The phone was just inside; I went back in and dialled our neighbours in the flat downstairs.

'Hello, Debbie?' I said, hopefully.

'No, Debbie's gone to work, can I help?'

I explained who I was; it transpired she, Mary, had just moved in. I went on to say how embarrassing this was but that I had a bird phobia and that there were currently several pigeons upstairs.

'I'll be right up,' she said.

I hovered nervously downstairs while she went up, and all was quiet for a long time.

'They've all gone!' she eventually shouted down.

'Are you sure?' I said. 'There are some drawers open in Jeremy's room, can you check they haven't gone in there?'

Silence.

'Pigeons don't make a habit of hiding in drawers,' Mary said, behind a laugh.

I pleaded I couldn't go up unless she was sure. She went into all the rooms, clapping her hands. Dripping in perspiration, I nervously went back upstairs to join her. I was impressed by her gentleness and patience.

'What do you do?' I asked.

'I'm a nurse,' she said.

I apologised about this being our introduction, and how the bird phobia seemed to make me a magnet for bird incidents, explaining that only the week before all this I had met a group of friends in the Slug and Lettuce on Hereford Road. It was a lovely spring day and we all sat outside under the trees with our drinks. Mid-conversation something fell from the tree and landed in my glass. As I focused, it bobbed up to the surface: a small pink embryo with a huge black eye, a beak and claws up around its face – more like a small dino-saur than a bird. I screamed. Someone took the glass and hurled the contents into the undergrowth. Mary laughed; 'Oh, don't worry,' she said, 'I once met some-one who was terrified of bananas.'

Perhaps the worst bird incident occurred when even-tually I moved out of Westbourne Terrace to live with Alice, the girlfriend I had met through Janet. Alice had gone away for the night, leaving me in charge of her beloved cats. Almost as soon as she had left on the Sunday morning, the male cat had identified a sick pigeon, which he skilfully corralled to the cat flap where it sat hunched and trembling. Convinced he was going to eventually bring it in through the cat flap, I tried to lock this from the inside, without success. I rang Alice. She laughed and said she was now too far away to come back, would I be all right? I assured her I would get the situation under control. I went out for the day.

A friend came round for supper, for which I was

grateful as the pigeon had gone and I needed to be sure the cat had not secreted it somewhere in the house. We drank rather a lot of wine and I slept deeply, but fitfully. I woke in the early hours and went for a pee. The corridor was narrow and we had sisal throughout. I blearily opened the loo door and realised there was some resistance – as I pulled it further open it scraped over a pile of what I assumed was cat sick. In the half-light I couldn't make it out and decided not to think about it until the morning. I went back to bed none the wiser.

In the morning I made my way along the corridor once more but as I came within sight of the loo I saw the most horrendous pile of flesh-coloured corpses, some sprouting small black feathers; there were splashes of blood up the door and the opposite wall and all over the floor.

As I focused from my paralysed position I realised that these were baby pigeons (squabs, as my girlfriend helpfully pointed out on her return). I was seized with panic. The cat must have found a nest and spent much of the night bringing them in; I had then opened the door over them. I retreated back to the bedroom, but with no exit from that end of the flat I would have to pass the horror in order to reach either the phone or the front door. Janet was upstairs, preparing to fly to LA later that morning as she had been nominated for an Oscar for her role in the film *Tumbleweed* (she lost out to Hilary Swank, who won for *Boys Don't Cry*).

The corridor was narrow enough and the carnage spread out enough that, in order to avoid any kind of contact, I would need to press myself against the wall, rather like Catherine Deneuve in *Repulsion*. I made a terrifying journey along the corridor, ending up on my hands and knees by the front door. It was 7.45 a.m. I phoned Janet. 'How are you with birds?' I said, a subject that had thus far in our friendship remained unexplored. 'Alive or dead?' she replied. 'Dead, in a horrific manner!' I replied. 'Can you ring someone else?' I said I would try my brother. 'Come back to me if he isn't there,' she said. I called Hodie's number, not hopeful as he had usually left for work by that time. To my enormous relief, he answered. He was in a hurry but would come over.

He made his way down the corridor, stood for a moment and then bent a little to look more closely. I can still see the shape he made as he straightened up; this was bad, even for him. He asked for a pair of rubber gloves and a plastic bag. 'Make that two!' he shouted after me. He removed the mangled corpses and then left hastily, telling me I would have to clear up. I spent the next half hour scrubbing blood off the walls and door and trying to get it out of the sisal. I still shudder to recall it.

'Morning, Tippi!' said Malcolm when I reached the office, rather pale.

# 26

## *A Doll's House*

O nce in a blue moon, the essential elements of a production come together like a coup de foudre. Thelma and I went to see Janet in a play at the Royal Court. We met in a pub afterwards and congratulated her on winning the Sony Award for her portrayal of Nora in Ibsen's *A Doll's House* on the radio. Janet had seen the production on stage several times but felt she had never seen it truly work. She told Thelma her ideas and said that she wanted to direct the play. Thelma said immediately, 'No, you must be in it. You must play Nora.' Janet thought this was ridiculous – she couldn't think of anyone less like a 'little skylark' than she was. 'Nobody would call me a little bird!' Nora is famously portrayed as diminutive, fragile. It took a couple more meetings before Thelma was able to persuade Janet that with the right director – one who found Janet's ideas for the play interesting – she simply had to play Nora.

The playwright Frank McGuinness agreed to do a version for us and we found our director in Anthony Page. When we began casting there was not a single agent who didn't express surprise that Nora was to be played by an actress who was over six feet tall. Our greatest challenge was to find an actor taller than Janet to play Torvald. Enter Owen Teale. Janet was 'a name' and respected, but not as well known as she would become later. We were going to have to do well on the tour to secure a West End theatre because no one would guarantee us a transfer on the basis of the actors we had.

Casting with Anthony Page was one of the most pleasurable experiences. He knew exactly what he wanted and he communicated it with such intelligence and wit that the process was as exciting as it was creative. Anthony was incredibly thoughtful and kind with actors during the audition process and this quality made me warm to him even more. When we were casting for an older woman to take on a non-speaking role and to also understudy, I saw him at his most gentle and sympathetic.

Several of the women I researched lived outside London. Thelma was strict that we did not pay train fares; they would have to come at their own expense, a situation which contributed further to my feelings of intense sympathy. I had told Anthony how I felt about this and explained that a few of the auditionees had made a considerable journey and so he gave them proper time, working them on stage, as he would any actor being seen for a speaking role. There was sometimes a pathos about these women that put one in mind of the lonely characters in a Jean Rhys novel. They would often be carefully, or in some cases not so carefully, made up and would obviously have gone to a great deal of trouble with their appearance. I would know almost instantly if they would not be taken on. However, we always made sure people were well looked after and treated with respect. No matter how busy we were, Thelma would make sure she attended as many of the auditions as possible.

Thelma was sure we had something special, and by the time we did a final run-through in the rehearsal room we all knew this for certain. The tour went very well, but still we had no London theatre, and despite Thelma's protestations none of the Avenue theatres were willing to take the risk. But when John Peter, then theatre critic for the *Sunday Times*, agreed to review the production on tour, we had some leverage. By this time, though, the theatres we hoped for were not available. Thelma eventually managed to secure the Playhouse Theatre on Northumberland Avenue. The reviews were unanimously brilliant. At number one in *Time Out* for a record six weeks, we had queues round the block. Thelma and I would walk down the lines of people, explaining that there was unfortunately no chance of them getting a seat for that evening's performance.

When Ibsen wrote the play in 1879 he said: 'A woman cannot be herself in modern society . . . [because it is] an exclusively male society, with laws made by men and with prosecutors and judges who assess feminine conduct from a masculine standpoint.' Janet's interpretation of Nora concentrated less on the feminist slant – maintaining that it's hard in the last scene to make that final conversion work if you come on like Emily Pankhurst, having been an idiot up until that point. She saw it more as the story of a marriage, of a flawed character and a flawed relationship. Many years later, Ibsen said that he 'must disclaim the honour of having consciously worked for the women's rights movement'.

What emerged through Janet and Owen's truly brilliant performances was an unsettlingly real and modern depiction of a marriage disintegrating, and of a woman growing apart from her husband. I swear I felt an air of conscious uncoupling as people left the auditorium in stunned silence.

\*

Whether a production is successful or not, the work involved is phenomenal. And for us the work didn't stop once a play had opened. We were always in pre-production for the next, and always looking after our plays once they were on. This meant being at the theatre at night, one or both or all of us. Although I came to believe that Thelma rather overdid this, I think she was right in that the producer's presence is a good thing and a positive addition to the overall dynamic. This doesn't mean performances are any better or worse, but it creates and maintain a sense of family and commitment to the piece that might not otherwise exist. As a result of this, I sometimes got very tired, and unlike Thelma I had to stagger home on public transport. Not earning enough money was fine up until I reached a certain age, but then it began to have a negative effect on my life.

Our joint achievement, of the three of us, was that mostly people believed our organisation to be far bigger than it was. When I look at the production credits in programmes now and see more than one of each of the following: Production Associate, Production Co-ordinator, Production Supervisor, Production Intern, Production Assistant – and that is without the producer and their assistant/s – I see us in a kind of sepia-toned past, like some odd Dickensian-type outfit. We were more careful with everyone else than we ever were with ourselves.

Another of Thelma's favourite phrases came into play during this time: 'The spirit of envy is alive and well in England.' It was strange how eagerly people would approach us in theatres when a play was struggling, or when we had received unfavourable reviews. The commiserating was almost gleeful. For some reason, when we were bathed in success few people said anything about it to our faces. But successful we were, and even the out-of-the-way theatre that nobody seemed to know how to find was full to the rafters. Janet won Best Actress at the Olivier Awards, and the Critics' Circle Award. Producer Bill Kenwright rang to say he wanted to take us to New York. He had the money and the American co-producer, we had the show, so it would be a mutually beneficial arrangement. On Broadway, *A Doll's House* won four Tony Awards. The *New York Times* critic, Ben Brantley, said of Janet's performance that it was 'the single most compelling performance I've ever seen on stage'.

This was my second visit to New York. I arrived the day before the awards and as the limousine drove me into the city, news of the singer Jeff Buckley's premature death was announced on the car radio. This time I shared a vast hotel room with Jeremy, one end of which was a huge wall of glass overlooking Times Square with a view so stunning I found it difficult to process. I imagined myself in *Blade Runner*.

Tom was then living in New York, so we spent an afternoon together. He had a habit of landing on his feet when it came to property and had found himself an apartment in a beautiful old building just round the corner from the Frick Collection. We walked around Manhattan and stopped for lunch somewhere by the river. It was hot and we drank white wine while watching a wedding party float past in an old wooden boat. I'd had just enough wine to feel my senses heightened, to feel sharper than I would have without it. Despite his stories of glamorous New York living, when I left Tom in his dark apartment before heading to Janet's to get ready for the big night, I sensed loneliness.

This time my clothes weren't quite so threadbare and my Issey Miyake outfit given to me by Ninagawa allowed me to float into Radio City Hall. As I watched Thelma follow Bill up on stage to receive the Award for Best Production, I realised how far we had come since that evening in a smoky pub in Sloane Square. My only sorrow was that Bill did all the talking and Thelma got to say nothing, despite the fact that it was truly her production. Though we wouldn't have been there without Bill's influence, given the play's undeniable feminist resonances, the irony was not lost on me.

After the awards ceremony we made our way to the dining tables. Janet and I smoked a cigar and somewhere there's a photograph of me sitting on her lap with very flushed cheeks, while she blows smoke rings into the air.

# 27

## Someone Will Play It

Casting disappointments were big in our office. We had wanted Miranda Richardson to play Ophelia, and when she came to meet Robert Sturua, for a moment I thought we had her, but we didn't. Having come up with what we considered a dream piece of casting, we would get excited, first when the agent was enthusiastic and then even more excited when it appeared that their client was close to accepting. But such courtship rarely got as far as 'walking down the aisle', as Thelma used to say, and just raised the bar for disappointment. Far better when they said no straight away. When we worked at the National, one of the older and more experienced women in the Casting Department used to say, when faced with yet another rejection, 'My dear, someone will play it.'

When Julie Christie considered playing Arkadina for us in *The Seagull*, the day she declined was terrible. I sat on the sofa in our office and stared into space. 'Would you please stop looking as though your entire family has been wiped out in a car accident!' Malcolm said. 'This is not open heart surgery!' He was right, of course, but for me the world in that office could easily become the world in its entirety, and I was never away from it for long enough to notice the increasing insularity.

We could become hermetically sealed off, rarely discussing anything other than our own 'world events'.

When we were in the middle of the second International-al Theatre season at the National, I had failed to notice the day the Berlin Wall came down. We were more like a small country than an office. Mourning the loss of Julie Christie, Thelma and I ended up in the Waldorf having dinner and getting a little drunk. We were asked to leave when we played the piano in the Palm Court, and had to be escorted from the building.

A day waiting for a major actor to say yes or no would involve continual questioning from Thelma. Though we'd give the agent a deadline by which we would need to know if their client was definitely *not* going to do it, we were always prepared to wait longer if there was a chance they *might* accept.

The call would come in to say that they were 'thinking about it', at which point the deadline would be extended and our hopes elevated. Thelma would sit in her leather chair and fiddle with her pearls, extend her hands in front of her and look at the rings on her fingers – she did this whenever deep in thought or bored rigid. It was always a bad sign during a play to see her looking down at her hands, admiring her rings.

Glancing to her right at the clock on the windowsill, which John Alderton and Pauline Collins had given her when she left the Theatre of Comedy, she would turn to me and demand to know why the agent had not called. The narrow windowsill tilted forward, and the clock regularly fell off when a heavy lorry or bus rumbled past Waldorf Chambers on the street far below, sending some strange vibration up the walls of the old Novello Suite. Somehow this rather tacky but much-loved clock (the clock face suspended in clear plastic embossed with a few garish coloured flowers, and surrounded by black and gold plastic) would crash to the floor but never break. Various cracks were held together by odd bits of Sellotape, and Malcolm had to add a piece of gaffer tape to hold the battery in place at the back. As Thelma continued to repeat at ten-minute intervals her demand to know why an agent had not called, we would get so fed up with hearing it that I'd refuse to make further calls. Malcolm would wait until she left the room and then he'd reset the clock, either to buy time or to speed it on, depending which course most benefited the situation.

One day Malcolm sent us out of the office to buy something for tea. We walked arm in arm through Covent Garden and ended up in Cranks, a vegetarian place Thelma never went to because 'It's not proper food, darling.' She bought flapjacks and handed over a twenty-pound note. The girl serving us gave her change for ten pounds. Thelma pointed this out, but the girl was adamant that Thelma had given her a ten-pound note. 'No,' I said, 'she gave you a twenty-pound note, I assure you.' Again the girl disagreed, at which point Thelma fixed her with a steely look and lowered her voice an octave. 'Do you know who I am?' she said, to which the pale, spotty and distinctly unflustered girl of course said no. 'I'm Thelma Holt!' replied Thelma, astounded by such impudence. We left with the right change.

We had already cast a twenty-six-year-old Michael Sheen as Konstantin in *The Seagull* and we were auditioning a handful of hot and promising young actresses for the role of Nina. We never saw rafts of actors for any one role, usually no more than six for each part. Robert Sturua was directing again, but this time we didn't have Helen, and the interpreter we used for the auditions had none of Helen's innate intuition or sensitivity around performers. It was thus harder to feel any connection being made between Robert and the actors during auditions and by the time one actress had emerged saying she felt as though she had been interrogated, followed by another who threw herself upon me in floods of tears, saying it was the worst audition she had ever had in her life, I knew it was time to fetch Thelma. She cancelled all her meetings and sat in on every audition from then on.

I had a young out-of-work actor helping me make cups of tea and coffee and seeing people in and out of the Strand Theatre, where we held the auditions. There was occasionally some light relief. 'What's that?' I said to my helper, pointing to something on the stage after we had just seen the last actress out, who happened to be a very hot young actress who had recently hit the big time with film. He came back with a script and a pair of pristine lacy black knickers. I asked him to take these back to the Donmar, where the actress was working, and leave them for her at reception. He wouldn't, until I put them in a brown Manila envelope. Even then, he was reluctant. We eventually cast another rising star, Kate Beckinsale.

This was a happy company; love blossomed between Kate and Michael and their bonhomie spread in all directions. Backstage at the Theatre Royal in Bath, they burst into the Green Room weighed down with shopping bags brimming with Michael's enhanced wardrobe, which had been strategically overseen by Kate. They were young, clever and good-looking. Creatively, it seemed the world was their oyster. This was perhaps the first time I admitted to myself that I was in a state of limbo. I knew acting was not for me, but was now less sure about being a producer. 'You'll be better at this than me, Pea, you are cleverer than I am,' Thelma had said to me on more than one occasion. But I didn't believe her. I didn't have her edge, her titanium-plated determination and unwavering belief in herself and her plans. Nor did I believe I had her skills in navigating what could be a brutal business.

This feeling of restlessness was highlighted by these young actors around me fulfilling their promise. Though I rarely got to visit any production on tour, whenever I did it intensified the feeling I'd have on returning to the office that my world was shrinking and that I wasn't creating anything.

Unfortunately for us, neither Michael nor Kate was at that point as famous as they would become, and without first-rate reviews we failed to secure a West End showing, so the production toured only. Not long after it was over, Michael and Kate came to see us in our tiny office and told us they were going to have a baby. Our egos were such that we felt personally responsible.

# 28

## *The Understudy*

Casting understudies I always found a very upsetting experience, particularly when dealing with the older character actor parts. There could be no illusions at this point about the actor's age, no possibility that they were working their way towards a successful career via any means. By the time an actor is in their fifties or sixties, it is clear that coming in for a non-speaking role to cover a leading actor, or even a supporting actor, perhaps getting the odd line or holding a spear, is not going to lead to anything better. When this procedure becomes competitive and only one of the group of actors being auditioned will get the job, the whole thing can be demoralising. Some directors do not even cast these parts, leaving that chore to an assistant, or in the old days, the company manager.

Only once did we find ourselves offering the audience their money back when a 'star' had to miss a performance. In a theatre with a capacity of just over a thousand seats, only forty people decided to stay for the performance. Usually a sick actor will have left the theatre long before curtain-up, if indeed they made it to the theatre at all. But as Thelma did her final rounds one evening, she heard sounds coming from the sick actor's dressing room. She opened the door to find him standing on a chair, his ear pressed up against the tannoy system, listening to his understudy's performance. 'Get down from there immediately! How could you? Go home now!' This was a serious breach of theatre etiquette.

A gifted understudy is a vital part of the smooth running of any production. When we found such people, we would hope to keep them in 'our stable', as Thelma called it. So always when casting we would call on these stalwarts to cover and play small roles, often without lines. Alan Haywood was one such actor, and he worked with us several times over the years. Alan collected Coronation glass, theatre programmes and other theatrical memorabilia from all the productions he had been involved with. He had made a life that worked for him, perhaps having accepted that this was his job, this was what he did. He absolutely loved the theatre. Always cheerful, well presented, totally reliable and a worthy man. In *The Clandestine Marriage*, he was understudying Nigel Hawthorne while also playing a small role.

Nigel not only starred in this production, he also directed it. The casting process was one of the most enjoyable, and working with Nigel turned out to be a true lesson and a real pleasure. The hardest part for us was his inability to be anything other than totally enthusiastic about every actor coming in to audition, resulting in each one leaving with the belief that they had the part. He wanted them all to have a role and found the decision-making a genuinely painful process. During our casting meetings, Nigel was very clear about what he wanted and would describe them physically as well as in character. We were trying to find a young unknown actress to play the ingénue in the piece – a recent graduate from drama school, perhaps. Suddenly he jumped up: 'Pea, look up so and so, she would be perfect!' I found her name in the index in *Spotlight* and turned to the page with her photograph. Thinking I had made a mistake, I searched the name again. 'What's the matter?' he said, noting my confused expression. When I showed him the photograph of an actress who was clearly the same age as he was, Nigel clasped his head in his hands and laughed. 'Darling, I only remember her as she was when we worked together forty-odd years ago!'

This happened often. He was a generous, funny and very private man. He and his partner Trevor lived in the country and had a driver who would collect Nigel from our offices and drive him home. We'd never worked with anyone who had their own driver. Thelma used a minicab service off Westbourne Grove that operated out of a launderette. Any deviation from the usual route direct to our office was problematic. 'Darlings, can you believe he didn't know where Fortnum & Mason was? I said just get me to Piccadilly and he asked where Piccadilly was!'

Nigel and Thelma had known each other for many years and I was to learn through her stories of their past that this now esteemed and 'grown-up' actor had a wicked and mischievous side. On the first day of rehearsals, we all gathered in a large rehearsal room, sat in a circle and introduced ourselves. Nigel then stood up to make a welcome speech and to thank everyone, including Thelma, Malcolm, the set designer and the costume designer. I thought I'd been forgotten but wasn't offended; he and I had worked so closely over the past weeks I could imagine him seeing me as an extension of his own furniture at this point. But he had saved his very special thank you to me until the end, and he really meant it; everyone clapped.

I suspect that when, over a vodka or two one night after the show, Thelma offered Alan a star-studded memorial in the event of his premature death, she did not imagine ever having to follow through with this promise. We were into the run, and the reviews, though not brilliant, were not so bad, and we were holding our own at the box office. I answered the phone one morning at 10 a.m. to Alan's agent. She had bad news, she said. Alan was dead. He had died that morning as he got dressed – a heart attack, she thought.

For Thelma it was business as usual; pragmatic as ever, she was straight on to Jeremy to get someone else ready for that night to cover the understudy. Nigel was immediately informed and that evening at the theatre the company were understandably sad and a little shaken. It was decided that evening's performance would be dedicated to Alan, so after the curtain had gone down everyone gathered in the Green Room to raise a glass. Everyone, that is, except Nigel. Thelma went off to fetch him from the dressing room, but returned alone. For Nigel it was very difficult losing his understudy; I believe fear more than anything else prevented him from being able to join in. Almost as though the death of his understudy – his stage 'shadow' – gave him intimations of mortality. It was a reminder of how insidiously superstition plays its part in the theatrical world.

A week later we got a call from Alan's partner, who told Thelma that Alan had spoken of her promise to arrange a memorial for him at the Actors' Church in Covent Garden. We were snowed under with work, in the midst of preparing for the next production. When she put the phone down Thelma said, 'Darling, we need this like a hole in the head.' But even at such short notice our actor friends were generous, including those who hadn't worked with him, or couldn't remember him. They all came along to read or say a few words. Alan Rickman had a very bad back and came in a taxi propped up like El Cid. Once again the house was full and it turned out to be a memorial most people would be very proud to have had, had they not been missing themselves.

With much flourish, Alan's partner presented Thelma, Malcolm and me with a bottle of champagne each in gratitude. In truth, he had little idea just how much effort had been expended by all concerned.

Sometime later I invited friends round to supper and thought how nice it would be for us all to have a glass of champagne. I opened Alan's well-chilled bottle and poured us all a glass. We raised our glasses. 'To Alan!' I said. We took a mouthful, looked at each other without swallowing and simultaneously spat out the contents. Alan had clearly collected bottles of stage champagne.

# 29

## *Sweetpea's Complaint*

The heady days of Westbourne Terrace were over.
It was no longer in the hands of the Dickens set;
Mr Gold had vanished and deals were being done that
were going to price us out of our home. Harry, Mark,
Polly, Felicity and the ever-changing cast of characters
downstairs had been gone a while. They were all now
married or living with significant others. Someone had
either bought their flat or signed a long lease, because
major works were in progress. The old brown wool
carpets were ripped up and filled a skip outside in the
terrace along with an assortment of 1970s fridges, television sets and comfortable chairs. I had moved into
the flat below Janet McTeer with Alice, Jeremy had
bought a flat, while Fifi too had joined the property
ladder. When we had finally emptied the flat of all our
belongings, Bronagh came to collect her 1960s sparkly
pink drum set. We had our own party and the girls from
*The Commitments* sang soul songs, and for once I didn't
care about the noise.

Not long after the move I got up one morning and
made my way the short distance to my brother and
sister-in-law's house. As I walked along, what had been
a slight discomfort in my bottom during the morning
became really painful. Hodie greeted me and followed
me down the hall. 'Why are you walking like that?' he
said. I explained that my bottom felt as though it was

full of broken glass, at which point he doubled up with laughter.

'What's so funny?' I said. 'It's really quite painful.'

'You've got a pile!' he said, before dissolving once more into fits of laughter, while Gigi, my far more sympathetic sister-in-law, tried to look concerned and not laugh.

'Don't be silly,' I exclaimed, 'of course I don't have piles – I'm far too young to have piles!'

'Do you want us to have a look?' they chirped in unison. My panic at the possibility of a pile was great, but not that great. 'How big do you think it is?' I said. Hodie opened a cupboard and riffled through some jars before producing a large borlotti bean, which he held up between his thumb and forefinger. 'About that size!' he said with glee.

I had no idea what to do about a pile. Gigi put her jacket on and set off for the chemist. She was a little reluctant to visit the nearest, as it had already been necessary to make three visits there that week. The first time was for ringworm cream, the second for a flea treatment, and the third for Canesten cream. She said that if she went in now and asked for Anusol he would wonder quite what kind of household she came from. She decided to go to the chemist's further on.

'How do you get piles?' I asked desperately. He explained they could be triggered by stress. 'I blame the Honey Monster,' he said. It was indeed a stressful time at Thelma Holt Ltd. I was very unhappy and had been for some time.

Gigi returned, bright red in the face. 'What happened?' we asked. It transpired that when she had reached the second chemist further away, having waited quietly at the pharmacy desk for assistance, a man suddenly stood up from behind the counter and to her horror she realised it was the same assistant who worked in the usual pharmacy – apparently this was his Saturday job. He didn't say anything when she asked for the Anusol.

A few days later, back at Hodie and Gigi's for supper with her parents, he took me aside and asked, 'How's the pile?' I explained that it was not really going away and that I didn't quite know how the cream was helping. Without hesitation he said that what I probably needed was an American preparation called Rectolube. Apparently he'd taken it upon himself to have a discreet word with Gigi's mother, a retired GP, and she'd agreed that this sounded like a very good idea.

The following day I ventured from the office at lunchtime and went first to Boots. I had decided that it was best not to whisper, but to simply ask for the stuff in a natural voice. 'Have you any Rectolube?' I asked the pharmacist. 'It's a preparation for piles.' He went away and looked through the shelves and then a book. There was now a queue forming behind me. He came back and said they didn't stock it, but that I should try the Garden Pharmacy in Long Acre. There, the assistant said no immediately and didn't need to look through the shelves to know that they did not stock Rectolube.

I continued slowly and uncomfortably down towards the Strand in the hope I could find another chemist, but to no avail. I had just decided to give up when my phone rang, it was Hodie asking me where I was and what I was doing. When I told him, there was a long silence. He managed not to laugh this time, but apologised profusely, saying he thought I realised that Rectolube didn't exist, it was all a joke.

# 30

## Hot Air

'How did you go bankrupt?' Bill asked.
'Two ways,' Mike said. 'Gradually and then suddenly.'
        *The Sun Also Rises*, Ernest Hemingway

During the summer in which Fiona played Richard
II at the National Theatre, she turned forty, and to
celebrate the occasion she'd invited a few close friends to
take a hot-air balloon trip with her. Because there were
two performances on a Saturday, this had to happen
during the week. I'd managed to negotiate with Thelma
for some time off the following morning, though it had
been an awkward conversation. Until that day I had
not understood the significance of my friendship with
Fiona – in particular, that it had marked the beginning
of new and creative horizons. I had been struggling to
find a rational way to articulate my growing desire for
autonomy, to begin a new and uncharted journey with
all the responsibility that would come from it.

We were all to meet at the stage door at 11 p.m. after
the performance and drive to Sussex to stay the night in
a B&B. The next morning at 5 a.m. we would leave for a
6 a.m. take-off, followed by a champagne breakfast and
then a dash back to London.

Among the ballooners accompanying Fiona were
Deborah Warner, Phyllida Lloyd and Stephen Daldry.

If there had been a disaster, then British theatre would have lost four of its finest talents in one hit. We drove in convoy and I shared a car with Stephen and Phyllida. I knew them a little, although I hadn't worked with either. Phyllida drove and I was leaning forward from the back seat, chatting to them both.

'What are you doing at the moment, Stephen?' I enquired.

'Well, I'm working on a film, actually.'

'A film!' we exclaimed excitedly.

'Yeah, it's about a boy from a housing estate who wants to go to ballet school . . .' He talked about the meetings he was having with the writer and the possible casting of Julie Walters as the boy's ballet teacher. I did wonder if the film would ever happen.

'What about you, Phil, what are you up to?' Stephen asked her.

Phyllida, who has a very calm and rather beautiful voice, replied, 'I've been asked to direct a musical in the West End based around the songs of Abba.'

Why on earth is she doing that? I thought.

We arrived at the house to find Fiona, her brother John, Deborah and the other guests already ensconced. It was late, but we all had a nightcap. The boys – Stephen, John and the others – sat up even later drinking whisky. It took me ages to get to sleep. My fear about the impending ascent had got out of all proportion, in an F. Scott Fitzgerald kind of way where 'at three o'clock in the morning, a forgotten package has the same tragic importance as a death sentence . . . ' The truth was, had it been anyone other than Fiona, I wouldn't have been there.

After about two hours' sleep we were up and off to

the balloon site. It was a beautiful morning and all the more vivid for the fugitive nature of the event. I was armpit-anxious, dizzy with my tumultuous inner self – I hate heights and all I had been thinking about was how crazy it seemed to be going up in what was essentially a large log basket. I shared my concerns with Phyllida as we wove our way down a lane and through fields to find our pilots. 'Oh, don't worry,' she said. 'They don't use baskets any more, they're solid sort of boxes, I've seen them – not sure what they are made of, but you can't see the ground through them and you are kind of gated in.' I felt a little comforted. But as we rounded the corner and entered the field there it was, and my stomach fell away. 'Phyllida! It's a fucking basket!'

We were given a lesson, mostly on what to do upon landing, which involves lying on your back with your feet up, holding on to the side of the basket. The holding-on bit proved to be the most useful information. Deborah Warner, who also suffers from vertigo, refused to be anywhere near the edge and placed herself firmly in the centre of the group. Once up, of course, it all seemed fine. Fear evaporated and a fleeting rush of the romance of it all, the views, the light and an overriding sense of privilege to be in this particular basket seized me. It's very quiet and though you see a lot, you don't hear anything, except for the occasional whoosh of flame firing the balloon. I watched a hare race around the perimeter of the field below, like a silent movie – interrupted occasionally by Deborah's enquiries about how things were at the edge. She never moved from her spot.

We seemed to be floating above a particularly affluent part of Sussex, as every property appeared to have a swimming pool, an outdoor horse school, or a private racetrack. 'Oh look,' said someone, 'isn't that Bryan Ferry's place?' The prospect of landing was the next worry, and not without reason as it turned out. It seemed to go on forever as we were dragged across a field full of bumps and the basket rolled over and over before coming to a halt up against a pile of old rubber tyres.

We all screamed.

By the time we got back to the house at about 8 a.m., the sun was already quite hot and we stood on a veranda with a glass of champagne, feeling high. In my case, the champagne merely exaggerated my overwhelming relief to be alive.

Breakfast began with half a grapefruit, which one member of the party decided needed a little seasoning. He liberally doused it with fine white powder – I think John thought this was sugar – before offering it to the rest of us. We declined, in the same polite manner one would decline condiments.

Stephen and I got a lift to the station to catch a train back to London. He slept his hangover off curled up on a seat, while I fretted about how much later I was going to be back in the office than I had promised Thelma.

# 31

## *Touch It and the Bloom Is Gone*

In the beginning, theatre excited and upset me in equal measure. My increasing knowledge of the scaffolding behind production and performance did nothing to diminish my appreciation of the magic. Sometimes I would emerge from the auditorium unable to speak. I was struck dumb in dressing rooms, unable to be very intelligent about what I had just seen, disarmed and disrupted by the power of performance. I'd watch actors take off their make-up and costumes and quickly transform from the larger-than-life character they had just been playing back to themselves, in all their magnificence or even ordinariness.

Thelma, meanwhile, never short on opinion, would rattle away – often contradicting everything she had said to me on the way backstage. And so she had taught me the very particular language of 'the dressing room'. 'If it's frightful, darling, never talk about the set or the costumes, always find something to say about the play and about their performance. There is always something positive to be found.' And she went on, 'Never say "Well done, darling!" or "You must be exhausted!" Never.'

What had been a gradual disenchantment had accelerated. It seemed that almost overnight the magic grew legs and arms and ran away screaming, 'It's all just an act, all of it!' Going to the theatre started to become a chore, all I saw was the scaffolding – on and off stage.

The novelty of smart restaurants had worn off too. Le Caprice, The Ivy, J. Sheekey, Orso . . . The late nights spent listening to affluent chatter amidst the clink and clatter of expensive tableware. Dimmed lighting and lowered voices sinking into padded banquets, dense tablecloths and heavy napkins. Walls lined with bad art, or black-and-white photographs of stars past who had passed. Nothing ever replaced the initial thrill that was my first trip aged nineteen to Joe Allen's theatre restaurant. That subterranean time warp where Thelma discovered that she hated eating salad out of wooden bowls, or anything off a wooden board: 'Full of germs, darling. How can they possibly get them clean!?' As the years went by, late nights in restaurants were hard work, and all I wanted was to go home. But I had been touched, and something had gone.

There was a time when London had seemed so contemporary, when the theatre I was helping to create seemed so avant-garde. This had now become history.

Fiona Shaw's grief-intoxicated Electra, Alan Rickman as Sei dying on the steps of a disused cinema in *Tango at the End of Winter*, Janet McTeer as Nora slamming the door and leaving her children behind at the end of *A Doll's House* . . .

Birds coming out of the bath taps, Thelma eating cat food by accident, a hot-air balloon landing in a field full of tyres. The real and imagined, the authentic and the pretend seemed indistinguishable.

There was a moment when it would have been the right time to leave, to take my new-found knowledge and find another challenge. But I thought I was having too much fun. I loved my work; I loved actors (mostly) and the non-judgemental environment we inhabited. It was an entertaining and sometimes dangerous world, and for a long time things were never dull.

Then there was Thelma, who in the beginning I found more interesting than anyone I'd ever met. There was no one like Thelma, and never will be. Her off-the-wall creativity and wit, her lack of constraint about almost anything, was like many doors simultaneously blowing open onto a brightly coloured new world, where anything was possible. And it was a world in which I was allowed to participate freely. But while staying too long at the fair I failed to notice for many years the toll on my development. The years rolled by, Hodie was running his own business. He and Gigi had their first child and bought a house.

Where was I? Another opening, another show!

When I thought about this too hard, I would dismiss it. It was frightening. I bumped into a director we'd worked with previously on my way out of the office one day: 'Why are you still working for Thelma? You're far too intelligent to still be here – you should get out!' This wasn't malicious, but I was embarrassed by my own lack of progress, unable to find the confidence to take a quantum leap away from what had always seemed like the right place. Admittedly, a financial safety net would have helped. I never had more than enough to scrape through to the end of the month, there was nothing left to buy me a bit of time.

The move out of Westbourne Terrace had proved to be the start of another kind of unravelling – the kind that is inevitable when you are serially broke. Suddenly it mattered because I was old enough to care about the limits on my existence and bored enough at work to understand that it wasn't worth it. Alice and I rented the ground floor of Janet's house for two years until she decided to buy the flat below her in order to extend her living space. Our knee-jerk decision was to buy a property together, although unfortunately our budget didn't extend to the increasingly salubrious Queen's Park. We moved a few miles up the road to Kensal Rise. My impecunious state dictated that this was a situation in which I had little control, and Alice took charge as she had the money for a deposit; consequently, my share in the property would be smaller, to reflect this. The flat and the street felt immediately alien, and unfortunately we'd picked a house with a drug dealer living above us. We came home one night to find what looked like an episode of *The Bill* in progress – the property taped off and surrounded by police cars. Our neighbour had been thrown out of the upstairs window.

Our time at Janet's had been happy domestically, but the move exposed our incompatibilities. We were on divergent paths, and inevitably began to drift apart. Although we tried to be kind to one another, for a while we made each other unhappy. Now my stomach was clenched both at home and in the office.

When one of my closest friends called one night in floods of tears, having just discovered she'd been cheated on, I told her to get in a cab and come over. I warned Alice of her extreme state of distress and asked her if she minded her staying the night. She didn't. The following morning my friend sat on our bed, still crying. I went to make tea for us all, and while I was gone, Alice slid further down the bed and said to my friend (affecting saucy voice): 'I'm naked under here.'

Not long after this illuminating incident, I turned up on Hodie and Gigi's doorstep in tears with a bag of clothes. They opened their door and a newly converted loft to me for as long as I needed it. I didn't have the money to rent anywhere else, I was still paying my share of the mortgage to my now ex-girlfriend.

Malcolm and I were alone in the office and I always told him everything. He never said very much about any of it. Information earthed with Malcolm and he understood things in a more profound way than the sharp-witted camp asides suggested. It was quiet so we were reading the *Evening Standard*. I spotted a piece about Sadie Coles having opened her own gallery. 'Look at this!' I said to Malcolm (Sadie had been a secretary in the Marketing Department when we were at the National). He read it, looked at me and said regretfully, 'What happened, Pea?'

I went to my parents' for the weekend, exhausted and unhappy. Work was joyless and uncomfortable and I was all at odds with myself with little idea what to do. I felt as though I had been at a strange academy for years and now found myself skilled in many ways but devoid of qualifications. It was true that there were no letters after my name; but the girl who used to paint freckles on her face and wear odd clothes could now cast a Shakespeare play, design a poster and negotiate an artist's fee with a tough agent. The girl too stunned to tell the star to take his hands off her tits was now someone he would have been too wise to approach in the first place. Monsters and madness left me unmoved. It had taken a long time to become a woman, and longer still to discover exactly what I didn't want to do.

That night, after turning out the light, I heard a scratching sound coming from the wooden stairs that led from my bedroom to an interconnecting door to the downstairs bathroom. I imagined it to be a bat in the roof or a mouse behind the skirting, and though I didn't like it, my tiredness won. But then it got louder, really loud. My heart was thumping so I put the light on and went to the top of the stairs. There was a mole scrabbling around on the wooden floor below, circling at the foot of the stairwell. I woke my parents. 'Oh, poor mole,' they chorused. 'Poppy [their adored cat] must have brought it in and let it go!' They showed no signs of getting up to fix the problem, so I said I was worried it would come into the bedroom.

'Moles don't climb stairs,' my mother said.

I lay in bed, listening to the mole.

# 32

## *Hold on Tightly, Let Go Lightly*

You are more useful to other people if you suffer from
vaulting ambition than you are to yourself.

Thelma Holt

I wonder if there are many very powerful women
genuinely able to promote the talent they have encouraged beyond the point at which it merely reflects
back their own glory. And if they could, if their solip-
sism wasn't so consistently triumphant, would they
be as potent and would their love be as savage and as
glorious. And if not, would the likes of me have endured
so long? I inhabited a world where the extraordinary
became commonplace, a world in which Thelma was
always the star protagonist and sometimes the monster.

There were signs that our golden age was over, but
there was a deficiency in me that would prolong the
acknowledgement.

What I admired most about Thelma also threatened
to dismantle the fabric of a guiding belief system
that had only previously been shaken by the outside
influences that had made it difficult for me both to
operate integrally as Thelma's 'creature' also to build
an identity of my own, one that would naturally lead to
independence. I had realised that this was not going to
be possible within the confines of Thelma Holt Ltd, and

in order to continue to be one of a pair of very high-class sidekicks, I would at least need to earn sensible money. But we weren't, nor had we ever been, in the sensible-money business. No one who worked in the theatre was in the sensible-money business. I had a feeling I had become the limited part of Thelma Holt Ltd.

I was torn between wishing to feel as 'liberated' as my freelance friends in terms of what appeared to me to be extended periods of freedom, and at the same time grateful that although my pay was a pittance it was at least a regular pittance. In the year 2000 I was taking home little over one thousand pounds per month and I was tiring of finding new ways to make a jacket potato exciting when the rent sucked up a good deal of that. I was being priced out of my life, and no amount of my-cup-is-half-full attitude could change the news in black and white each month on my bank statement. What on earth was I doing?

Nobody close to me in that world had experienced anything similar. My friends in the business had all faced the feast-or-famine nature of things that is par-ticular to the industry, but most had houses – some had more than one – they had cars, pension plans and exotic holidays. I still rented, couldn't afford proper holidays and had no pension plan. 'Darling,' Thelma had said one night in a taxi – in the same tone of voice that in-dicated she was about to state an indisputable truth I had not been quick enough to spot – 'you don't need a pension plan!' As far as she was concerned, my pension plan was the company and she hoped that I would go on running it when she, or fate, decided it. Even if the seeds of doubt had not been germinating long before this moment, I knew Thelma well enough to be aware that I would have to do at least another twenty years before this would happen.

The truth was that I was unsure about everything. My frustrations at not being closer to the creative process should have signalled this to me sooner. In order to indulge in all the things that fascinated me, the magic of plays coming to life in the hands of great actors and directors, someone had to pay. I wasn't interested in the phenomenally difficult business of raising money, doing deals with theatre landlords and artists' agents. I didn't want to tell directors they couldn't have the budget they wanted in order to make their vision come to life.

This was hard to acknowledge. What, if not this, was I to do? How could I explain to myself, or indeed anyone else, why it seemed the last twenty years were about to prove to be another kind of cul-de-sac?

I felt physically sick the morning I asked to talk with Thelma alone. How do you tell someone you have spent more time with in the last two decades than you have with any lover or family member that you think it's over? She was typically robust about it, and when I explained that the main reason was an economic one – that I knew there wasn't the money available to pay me the kind of salary that would make sense – she said, 'But, darling, you're famous!' I said, 'Thelma, I am being serious!' But she knew I was serious, she also knew that the reason wasn't entirely financial. Something was broken and would never get back into a shape we both recognised.

We spoke for some time; there was no bad blood between us, and I felt that although she wasn't saying so, she would probably have preferred that I stayed. She knew I was planning to travel and that I wanted to buy a camper van to drive around Europe for my very late gap year – or as Thelma came to refer to it, 'your little wank'.

We began negotiating a sensible date for me to leave. This took some time. We both stood before the year planner on the wall behind her chair. Thelma continually moved the date – each time I suggested what I thought was a sensible time she would say, 'Well, you've got to do the Japanese, darling – Ninagawa will be so disappointed if you don't.' And then, 'Well, don't you want to stay to do the preparation for Bergman?' By the time we had finished our chat, I was working out a year's notice.

The other slight complication for me was that she didn't want anyone outside the office to know. 'Darling, everyone will think we've fallen out.' This was ironic, charming, but absurd. My concern was that if nobody knew I was leaving, if I just suddenly wasn't there – well, that might really look as if we had fallen out. What on earth would people think? I imagined many would think that I'd had a nervous breakdown. She rummaged about among the papers in her in-tray. 'Where are my pissing glasses, Pealet?' I found them and gave them to her. The rummaging continued and then she handed me a cheque, enough money for me to buy the camper van.

# 33

## *The Last First Night*

On 3 April 2003 I made my way to our office in Waldorf Chambers for the last time. Thelma and I often travelled in together, but we didn't that morning. She had gone in a people carrier to collect six large boxes each containing twenty-five chocolate rabbits – she had done a deal with Thorntons who had over-ordered for Easter.

After lunch I walked over Waterloo Bridge to the National Theatre to prepare for the opening performance of Yukio Ninagawa's all-Japanese production of *Pericles*. The view from there is always pretty spectacular, London at its best, and when bright and sunny, as it was that day, it can make you heady with ambition. I was full of nostalgia, remembering all the times I had walked over that bridge checking out the old Ceefax sign that advertised the day's performances for each of the three theatres, and the thrill I got the first time I saw Peter Stein's *The Hairy Ape* in lights all those years previously. But there was blankness to this day as well – that's what felt so heightened – the blankness.

Halfway across the bridge, something caught my eye in the road to my right. At first I thought it was a pannier that had fallen from someone's bicycle, or a bag dropped from a bus. As I got closer I realised it was an animal, a dead animal. Cars were swerving to avoid it.

Closer still and I could see a tail, long and thin. It was a rat, a rat the size of a cat.

I arrived at the stage door; this time there were no butterflies in my stomach and I could find my way around the building blindfolded. Linda was setting out the trestle tables that used to be put up for every first night so that the cast could leave each other gifts. She had been sitting all morning writing out over eighty name cards for the Japanese cast and crew. I negotiated the maze of corridors to the dressing room that had been assigned to us for use as an office. Nicholas Hytner was now running the National and it was no secret that he no longer wanted to present foreign work, so it was the end of many things for us that day.

I would spend the next couple of hours, with the help of a volunteer, attaching cards with messages of thanks from Thelma, Malcolm and myself to each rabbit, and having them delivered around the building to every department who had in some way been involved, from the stage door to the press office to the technicians. We had learnt early on the importance of these small gifts.

In the very first International Theatre season Thelma had bought, as presents for the company, sacks full of furry toys going cheap from a toyshop that had gone into receivership. When by some oversight a technician called Jim Hancock (one of 'the heavies', as Thelma referred to them) didn't receive one, the sight of him at our office door covered in tattoos with tools hanging from his belt, announcing in a somewhat threatening manner that he hadn't got his teddy bear, was enough to ensure rigorous checks in the future.

In the beginning we used to call the National 'The

Bunker'. But I fell in love with the brutalism of the architecture of the building and with its utilitarian ambience. It had a left-over-from-the-1970s feel about it, a little ragged around the edges. The weight of the doors, the width of the corridors, the walls lined with framed posters from past productions, the thin industrial carpets in our offices, the old lifts that rumbled, the stairwells that echoed throughout the centre of the building, and the smell – 'Smells are surer than sounds or sights to make your heartstrings crack,' said Rudyard Kipling. Even now, when I visit, that smell can transport me back twenty-seven years. I can recall the vivid and heightened way in which I experienced things then. I absorbed everything without judgement, and with the innocence that youth confers upon one.

A lot of people still didn't know I was leaving Thelma, but the few who did kept appearing with cards, gifts and farewell hugs. Alan and Rima came with beautiful flowers. 'Safe voyage, oh great one,' said Alan's witty card. Nigel Hawthorne's partner, Trevor, was there with a gift from him and Nigel (in absentia). His death was still so recent Trevor could hardly speak of him without tears in his eyes.

As soon as the curtain had gone up, Malcolm, Thelma and I went to the Mezzanine Restaurant and had supper. I remember little about it, except a sense that emotion should be bottled for now. I don't think Malcolm even stayed for the party, and when we said goodbye it was as though we were going to be seeing each other at ten o'clock the following morning, as usual. He had never expressed affection towards me in any obvious way, but I believe he was fond of me and perhaps even respected me for leaving.

*

I'd had the best mentor, and had been superbly groomed in a job many would have killed for. Perhaps this world could have been my oyster, but I just didn't want it. I wasn't frightened by not knowing what to do next, Thelma had given me everything I needed; her enormous presence had enabled knowledge – and it was far greater than was apparent in that moment.

Thelma and I did our bit at the party, which with one exception was like every other first-night party had been at the NT. A woman approached us and appeared at a distance to be wearing a Vivienne Westwood outfit – that's what I thought at a glance and I'm fairly confident Thelma did too. She smiled widely at us and Thelma began to move towards her, as if she knew her, and for a moment I thought she did, extending her arms in a greeting, just as I noticed that the Vivienne Westwood was in fact a mirage; the reality – bundles of material and bags in layers, and even before this, or perhaps at the same time, the sudden and overwhelming stench of ammonia. 'Oh dear,' said Thelma under her breath as quickly as she changed course, and at that moment a technician and a stage manager swept in and gently escorted the many-layered bag lady out of the building.

Alan wanted to take us out to supper. Thelma declined and I felt it necessary to make the evening more about her than me. If we didn't make much of my leaving, perhaps I wasn't really leaving after all. We got into a taxi and she dropped me in Queen's Park on her way home.

As I watched the taxi recede I could still see Thelma, bent forward, her head lowered as she searched for something in her Hello Kitty bag. For a moment I imagined her selecting some of the relics of our past and laying them out beside her: a pair of heavy-rimmed spectacles, a stick of Dior No. 21 lipstick, an old envelope covered in figures, a packet of urgent biscuits.

I turned towards home, the small black box held tightly in my hand.

# Acknowledgements

My sincere thanks to Fiona Shaw for her unshakeable friendship and for all the adventures, not least the trip that set this book on its course. If she hadn't made such terrible porridge I wouldn't have been so eager to get to my desk.

To Caroline Michel, my brilliant agent – this book just wouldn't exist without her.

Anne Robinson for her wit, wisdom and for always being right.

Michael Foster for his unfailing support and generosity.

Alan Samson and Simon Wright at Weidenfeld and Nicolson, for your superior editing and for looking after this beginner so kindly.

My particular thanks to Rosie Beattie, Penny Wesson, Patricia Routledge, Janet McTeer, Nelle Andrew at Peters Fraser and Dunlop, Phyllida Lloyd, Deborah Warner, Ernie Hall and Jeremy Adams.

Thank you, Thelma and Malcolm, for the journey.

Eternal thanks to my inner cabinet: Hodie and Gigi, and my nephews Theo and Cosmo, Paloma ('Why can't I be a nephew?'), Fifi Tutton, Bronagh Gallagher, Anna Niland, Kate Hubbard, Harriet (Harry) Wallace Sewell, Ellie Sturrock and Karen Robertson, who also happens to be the best osteopath in the country.

To the great love in my life, Kate. For her unique perspective, and for making me cry with laughter.

To my parents Lesley and Nigel Slight, for everything, *everything*.